"There's nothing [...]
every morning a[...]   p
partner with the [...]   o
is a wonderful way of 'making it your ambition to be pleasing to him.'
And I'm so excited that David Powlison shows the reader how to do just
this in his remarkable new book *How Does Sanctification Work?* I give it
a hearty thumbs-up!"

> **Joni Eareckson Tada,** founder and CEO, Joni and Friends
> International Disability Center; author, *A Spectacle of Glory* and
> *Beside Bethesda*

"Every Christian leader, writer, or pastor should have David Powlison
whispering in his ear, 'God's Word is deep and rich . . . don't just sit on one
paradigm—teach the full counsel of God.' This book will do that for you."

> **Paul Miller,** executive director, seeJesus; author, *A Praying Life* and
> *A Loving Life*

"To know David Powlison is to know a man who is growing in the sweet
fruit of sanctifying grace. To witness his ministry is to see one whom the
Lord is using to sanctify many. That is why I am so grateful for *How
Does Sanctification Work?* One of the most crucial areas of debate among
Christians today concerns the doctrine of sanctification. David's is a voice
of sound, biblical wisdom in the midst of much confusion. If you are looking for a book on sanctification that is profoundly personal, biblically
balanced, and deeply relevant, then this is it."

> **Heath Lambert,** associate pastor, First Baptist Church of
> Jacksonville; executive director, Association of Certified Biblical
> Counselors; author, *A Theology of Biblical Counseling* and
> *Finally Free*

"In this book, David Powlison sets out a case against simplistic statements
that sanctification can be reduced to a 'just do this' or 'just believe that'
kind of process. Doing what he always does so brilliantly, he shows us how
the riches of Scripture get applied to the details of life. Personal, practical,
and bursting with fresh and important insights, here is a book to help God's
people become more like Christ."

> **Steve Midgley,** executive director, Biblical Counselling UK; senior
> pastor, Christ Church Cambridge

"When I think about wise men who have shaped my life and thinking, David Powlison consistently rises to the top. His thoughtful and incisive insight into the human heart and what makes sanctification work is something each of us desperately needs. David recognizes that for all the conversation and writing which have taken place on the topic of sanctification, what seems to be left out is *you*! David helps bring his personal story and others' narratives into the discussion surrounding sanctification, and in so doing reminds us of the multifaceted way God *works* in people's lives. Grab this book today, read it and soak it in, and join David and many others in the process of becoming more like our Savior."

Jonathan Holmes, pastor of counseling, Parkside Church, Uniontown, Ohio; author, *The Company We Keep: In Search of Biblical Friendship*

"*Sanctification* is a very long word. Though many Christians would be able to give a simple definition such as 'growing in holiness' or 'becoming like Jesus,' few have given much thought to the dynamics of how it happens—how it works. In *How Does Sanctification Work?*, Powlison helpfully identifies five ways our growth in holiness happens. The principles are grounded in Scripture and illustrated by a transparent look at how it has 'worked' in his own life. And this is an encouragement for us to see how it—no, how *God's Spirit*—is at work in our lives, too."

Timothy Witmer, professor of practical theology, Westminster Theological Seminary; pastor, St. Stephen Reformed Church, New Holland, Pennsylvania; author, *The Shepherd Leader* and *The Shepherd Leader at Home*

"Sanctification is essential to fulfilling our greatest calling in life: namely, to love God with all our hearts and love our neighbors as ourselves. David has not only set forth the essential themes of this process but also described many of the spiritual nuances that guide our steps through this blessed transformation."

Ken Sande, founder, Peacemaker Ministries and Relational Wisdom 360

"Sanctification is a life-and-death matter. What David Powlison offers in this book is no mere how-to manual on having your quiet time. Instead, behind this straightforward title lies an explosively powerful and practical theology of human transformation. This book is deep enough to instruct those who have spent their lives agonizing over how sanctification really works, and accessible enough to guide those who have never had the question cross their minds. In short, this book will leave you fundamentally changed for the better."

Alasdair Groves, director of counseling, CCEF New England

HOW DOES SANCTIFICATION WORK?

DAVID POWLISON

WHEATON, ILLINOIS

How Does Sanctification Work?

Copyright © 2017 by David Powlison

Published by Crossway
    1300 Crescent Street
    Wheaton, Illinois 60187

Cover design: Kevin Lipp

Cover image: Shutterstock

First printing 2017

Printed in the United States of America

Trade paperback ISBN: 978-1-4335-5610-4
ePub ISBN: 978-1-4335-5613-5
PDF ISBN: 978-1-4335-5611-1
Mobipocket ISBN: 978-1-4335-5612-8

Library of Congress Cataloging-in-Publication Data

Names: Powlison, David, 1949– author.
Title: How does sanctification work? / David Powlison.
Description: Wheaton : Crossway, 2017. | Includes bibliographical references and index.
Identifiers: LCCN 2016035995 (print) | LCCN 2016040166 (ebook) | ISBN 9781433556104 (tp) | ISBN 9781433556111 (pdf) | ISBN 9781433556128 (mobi) | ISBN 9781433556135 (epub)
Subjects: LCSH: Sanctification—Christianity. | Spiritual formation.
Classification: LCC BT765 .P69 2017 (print) | LCC BT765 (ebook) | DDC 234/.8—dc23
LC record available at https://lccn.loc.gov/2016035995

Crossway is a publishing ministry of Good News Publishers.

DP   27   26   25   24   23   22   21   20   19   18   17
15   14   13   12   11   10   9   8   7   6   5   4   3   2   1

To Paul Miller—
faithful friend, wise counselor,
and mere Christian

CONTENTS

INTRODUCTION

At the close of his Gospel, John stands back and considers all that he has witnessed over a lifetime: "Now there are also many other things that Jesus did. Were every one of them to be written, I suppose that the world itself could not contain the books that would be written" (John 21:25). I love the juxtaposition of those two sentences. The fact that John left out innumerable stories prompts a cosmic leap of insight and imagination. He has just finished a sixteen-thousand-word book—slightly shorter than the short book you are holding. But the *whole earth* could not hold all the *other* books that could be written about what Jesus did!

What would all those unwritten books say? We know with certainty that they would contain the same *kinds* of things as the book that John did write. His Gospel largely consists of scenes selected from Jesus's encounters and conversations with various followers, foes, inquirers, and "undecideds." John gives glimpses into the life stories of different people as their lives intersect with Jesus. We do not witness Jesus's life story in isolation from other people. His loving actions are not a theological abstraction. We learn of Jesus by seeing and hearing how he interacts with others. Those countless books that could be written would tell of innumerable personal encounters.

When did all these other things take place? Some stories John left out were about encounters before Jesus ascended. And the unwritten books would include what the Spirit did in carrying Jesus's work forward during the subsequent fifty years of John's life—things he witnessed personally, things he heard from other people, and things he never knew happened because they occurred outside his purview. And, no doubt, these books would also tell all that the Lord is continuing to do ever since John's death. The unwritten books would include your story and mine.

And why are there so many possible books, and why are the books so voluminous? The world cannot contain life stories of events more numerous than grains of sand on the seashore. The details matter. Every person, in every circumstance, in every moment displays never-to-be-repeated specifics. God considers them all—every careless word, every hair on your head, every tear. What Jesus does in each of our lives works with the particulars.

Amid this variety there are commonalities, of course. The common denominator is Jesus Christ and how he works out his saving, sifting, sanctifying purposes. But the variety of personal stories is as significant to God as the common themes. The unique moments are the touch points where the Lord gets specific. So as John writes about the Lord, the camera repeatedly zooms in, slows everything down, lingers on a snippet of conversation, notes a situational detail. John (like all the Gospel writers) invites us to watch Jesus interact, person by person, situation by situation. He invites us to notice how and what Jesus notices. He lets us hear the questions Jesus asks, and how he answers those who question him. We learn how Jesus sizes up people. We watch how he finds the point of engagement, and then how he enters in, reacts, helps, rattles, invites, irritates, teaches, argues, clarifies, perplexes, saves, warns, encourages. When Jesus crosses paths with you, he reveals you for who you are. He precipitates decisive choices. In response to him, people change, either making a turn for the better or taking a turn for the worse.

Whenever a person makes a turn for the better, *sanctification* is happening. That five-syllable word which forms part of the title of this book needs some defining. What are we talking about when we ask, "How does sanctification work?" First, to be most accurate, we are discussing *progressive sanctification*. Like the word *save*, *sanctify* has a past tense, a present tense, and future tense:

- In the past tense, your sanctification has already happened. You are a saint—an identity for which you get no credit! God decisively acted by making you his very own in Christ. You have been saved.
- In the present tense, your sanctification is now being worked out. God is working throughout your life—on a scale of days, years, and decades—to remake you into the likeness of Jesus. You are being progressively sanctified. You are being saved.
- In the future tense, your sanctification will be perfected. You will live. Your love will be perfected. You will see God's face when he decisively acts to complete his work

> of conforming you to the image of Jesus. You will par-
> ticipate in the glory of God himself. You will be saved.[1]

That present-tense inworking of faith and outworking of love is the focus of this book. But we should always bear in mind that what God is doing now in your life builds on what he has done and leads to what he will do.

Second, the words *sanctification*, *saint*, *holy*, and *holiness* frequently conjure up a variety of odd, hyper-spiritual images. But these words intend to communicate earthy, practical realities. To be sanctified is to have your faith simplified, clarified, and deepened. You need God. You know God. You love God. You see life, God, yourself, others more truly. And to grow as a saint is to grow in actually loving people. How other people are doing matters increasingly to you. You care. You help.

Becoming more holy does not mean that you become ethereal, ghostly, and detached from the storms of life. It means you are becoming a wiser human being. You are learning how to deal well with your money, your sexuality, your job. You are becoming a better friend and family member. When you talk, your words communicate more good sense, more gravitas, more joy, more reality. You are learning to pray honestly, bringing who God really is to the reality of human need.

And to grow in holiness does not mean you now talk in hushed tones and every third sentence quotes the Bible. It means you live in more clear-minded hope. You know the purpose of your life, roll up your sleeves, and get about doing what needs doing. You are honestly thankful for good things. You honestly face disappointment and pain, illness and dying.

Sanctification, *saint*, *holy*, and *holiness*—they speak of daily life. There is nothing more practical than to live with an ever-growing love, joy, and purposefulness. There is nothing more eyes-open and helpful than to be maturing in wisdom, hope, and faith.

These two clarifications of the language of sanctification are meant to help us keep oriented. Clear-minded, true theology tracks the big themes. But most of this book will come down to street-level living. The variety, freshness, and complications of stories are what make the Gospels, life, people, and ministry so interesting. The details make both your life and God's Scripture interesting. The details matter because Jesus finds each one of us in our particulars.

And it is noteworthy that, in finding us, Jesus never ministers by rote. Because people and circumstances are not clones, there is no boilerplate in his conversations, friendships, or preaching. No distilled formula. No abstract generalizations. No "Just do x" sorts of advice. Because situations and persons come un-scripted, fluid, and unpredictable, Jesus engages each person and situation in a personalized way. It is no truism to say that Jesus really does meet you where you are. Always. Scripture does the same. No boilerplate. The Holy Spirit makes words personal.

This book will revel in the *variety* of how Jesus Christ works to change lives. And it will probe in order to establish the deeper *patterns* that are operating within all the variations.

The chapters that follow will drill down into how growth in grace actually works, and thus how ministry works to pro-mote growth. I will interweave personal stories and exposition. The Christian life can be expressed biographically or described theologically. Both have their place, and ideally they come hand in hand—as they do in the Bible! Scripture weds stories and interpretation, and I hope that my attempt to do likewise will prove faithful to the message and the method of Scripture, and helpful to you.[2]

1

GOD MEETS US WITH
HIS PROMISES

Let me begin by telling a story about events so familiar as to seem unremarkable. Yet it mirrors the experience of innumerable Christians who find the Word of God coming to life. Like making a Skype connection, or like an antibiotic healing bronchitis, the apparently mundane appears almost miraculous when you think about it.

In the Bleak Midwinter

This morning my wife, Nan, and I were each feeling mildly overwhelmed by the pressures of life. The family had succumbed to various combinations of flu, bronchitis, pneumonia, and head colds over Christmas. A week later, both of us still felt half-sick and weary. On top of this, we were pressed by a weight of concern for an elderly loved one battling intractable, deteriorating health problems. Nan faced a swarm of decisions and projects arising from a kitchen renovation, and I was deep in snowdrifts of overdue grading, correspondence, and writing projects. The net effect? We were both beset with that most endemic of human disorders: a nameless mash compounded of stress, distraction, preoccupation with responsibilities, ambient anxiety, incipient irritability, and complaint. Neither of us entered the day as a flourishing garden of love, joy, peace, or patience.

We needed sanctifying this morning—as we do every morning. And God met us with gifts of his Word and Spirit. He refreshed us, giving us what we needed. How? What brought renewal? We happened to be reading a passage from the farther reaches of Deuteronomy:

> [The LORD] found [Jacob] in a desert land,
>   and in the howling waste of the wilderness;
> he encircled him, he cared for him,
>   he kept him as the apple of his eye.
> Like an eagle that stirs up its nest,
>   that flutters over its young,
> spreading out its wings, catching them,
>   bearing them on its pinions,
>   the LORD alone guided him. (Deut. 32:10–12)

What happened? The Lord wrote these words on our hearts, as he promises he will do (Jer. 31:33). Here in a suburb of Philadelphia, on an early January day, the Holy Spirit took hold of things written down long ago. He clarified our minds, reawakened our faith, and animated our obedience. What happened pointedly illustrates how these words in Deuteronomy were "written down for our instruction" (1 Cor. 10:11; see also Rom. 15:4).

Nan picked up on the first half of the passage. She put her immediate response this way: "When you feel like a castaway who needs to be found and rescued, to be treated as 'the apple of his eye' means the world to me. The Lord encircles me. The Lord cares. The Lord watches over me. I'm not alone." She perked up. Her prayers and plans for the day came to life. She made good choices through her day.

My response was similar—but, no surprise, with a nuance of difference. The image of God's people trekking through the desert resonated both metaphorically and literally. It connected a vivid image—"the howling waste of the wilderness"—to my sense of living amid a swarm of pressures. And it evoked significant memories of hiking through California's Anza-Borrego Desert in 115-degree heat during the 1980s. Similarly, the image of being encircled with protective care, like an eagle fluttering over its nest, resonated with me. I've seen ospreys do that. The Lord encircles, hovers over, and carries his beloved people—and I am one of his. Troubles, temptations, and our God came together. Like Nan, I went into my day with a clearer sense of purpose, a more focused mind, and more attentiveness to others.

That day, in a small way, the Lord changed how we lived. Each of us, and both of us together, found what we needed. He comforted our hearts and established each of us in today's version of "every good work and word" (2 Thess. 2:16–17). We needed sanctifying; the Spirit sanctified us.

How Many Are His Ways

It was a textbook example of the innumerable ways God speaks and works. The words he used this time to meet us in our need surprised us. I'd never been struck by this particular passage. Though I'd no doubt read it many times, it formed no part of my conscious Bible knowledge. These particular promises and metaphors had never "popped" for either of us. Were there thematic similarities with how God's hand, Scripture, and life experience intersected on other days? Certainly. But this was a fresh encounter on a new day.

I am convinced that our understanding of the process of the Christian life is greatly enriched by considering multiple mundane examples, both in Scripture and in our lives. The pages that follow will look from many angles at how God changes people.

The actual unfolding of progressive sanctification is no theoretical topic. One interesting characteristic is that all Christians already have at least some firsthand experience. Every Christian can say of some person, passage, or event that God used, "*This* was key in helping me when I was struggling with *that* in *those* circumstances." The stories are indeed varied![1]

But firsthand experience also presents a danger. It is tempting to extrapolate a general rule from your own experience: "This must be the key for everyone." Both Scripture and personal testimony teach us that there is no single formula for the kinds of problems that call for sanctification. There's no one-size-fits-all goal. No sound bite captures the range of truths that shape change. There's no one blueprint for the constructive influence of other people. There is no single formula for how God weaves together the turns of events, the intricacy and beauty of his creation, the rich portrayals of life in literature and the arts—all things.

Multiple stories help us realize that not everyone is like us. Are there common denominators? Yes. But to become a general rule, the underlying patterns must be of the sort that adapt well and flexibly to a multiplicity of cases. I will seek to do justice to both the variety and the commonality of factors God uses in our sanctification.

2

IS THERE ONE KEY TO SANCTIFICATION?

We are all tempted to oversimplify. We long for one "key" truth, a "secret" principle, the foolproof technique, some life-changing experience that makes everything different from now on. If only there were some one thing to make Christian growth certain! But there is no single key.

"Just . . ."

You often hear people say things like "He should just remember that . . ." Or "If only she would just do . . ." Or "If I could just experience . . ." You've probably said things like that yourself. I certainly have. Preachers, teachers, counselors, authors, and friends instinctively gravitate toward naming some truth, some spiritual discipline, some action step, or some experience as the key that will unlock everything. The phrase "Just . . ." is a tip-off. But there are no "Just [do x, y, or z]" solutions to the puzzles of our sanctification.

This book does not arise in a vacuum. Like you, I've heard monochromatic, singular, one-size-fits-all messages telling me how I can grow in the grace and knowledge of the Lord Jesus Christ. Theological fads and fashions come and go. Here's a selection of perennial candidates that tempt us to think, "*This one thing is the secret key that will unlock your Christian life!*"

1. Remember that *God is sovereign* and is working all things for good in those who love him. The meaning of your troubles changes as you realize that he has called you into his saving purposes in Christ.
2. Rehearse and remind yourself of your *identity in Christ*. Union with Jesus Christ is the anchor of your salvation. All other identities are secondary.
3. Make sure you are in honest *accountability relationships*. None of us is meant to bear our burdens alone. God so works things that we can truly help one another as servants of Christ.
4. Avail yourself of the *means of grace*. Sit under good preaching, participate in corporate worship and sacraments, and maintain daily Scripture reading and prayer. To flourish, you need truth that is in Jesus to fill your heart.
5. Wage *spiritual warfare* against the predator of your soul. Clothe yourself in Christ. Put on God's weaponry of faith and love. Resist the enemy's lies, accusations, temptations, and aggressions.

6. Get busy *serving* others with the gifts the Lord has given you. Get out of yourself. Do something constructive with your life today.
7. Remember that you are accepted by God as his child and that he fully forgives your sins through the shed blood of Jesus. *Past grace* affirms that God is forever for you.
8. Ask the Lord to give his Holy Spirit that you might walk in his ways. *Present grace* daily strengthens you in the reality that God is with you.
9. Set your hope fully on the grace to be revealed at the revelation of Jesus Christ. *Future grace* carries you forward through affliction because God will come for you.

Every one of these tells us something true and good. Each highlights a facet of the many-splendored gospel of Jesus. We need every one of these things—and many other things as well. These nine assertions become problematic only when we lapse into saying, "Just remember this one thing . . . Just rehearse . . . Just make sure . . . Just ask . . . If you will just do . . . "

Our nine items capture some of the promises, revelations, purposes, commands, perspectives, providences, and helps that our God reveals in revealing himself to us. None of these stands supreme, relegating the others to the shadows. None of these is magic. And you could never remember all of these at any one time. Not one of them means the end of the struggle—not even all of them put together. They speak in different ways to how we struggle. And the Lord makes different truths meaningful at different times to different people.

Notice something else about the nine truths. I've framed each of them a bit abstractly. No eagles hover over eaglets. No people wander through the desert wondering what awaits them on the other side of that river. We hear no conversations, feel no emotions, and watch no particular struggle unfold. These truths and exhortations—wise truths, helpful exhortations—have been taken out of context. As propositions, they have been stripped of the names, places, experiences, failures, successes, dramatic actions, and vivid metaphors that clothe most biblical revelation. They will need to be brought back into the here and now. You and I need each one of these truths—and many more—to be reclothed and to walk on the ground where we walk.

We need stories and word pictures, both from Scripture and from the testimonies of daily life. We need to understand how Scripture illumines and connects to our current situation. We need practical help to work out the implications and applications for who we are, for where we struggle, for what we face. We need Jesus to be present—the Lord who is my Shepherd, the Lord who watches over my going out and my coming in. Scripture vividly and inductively demonstrates how these truths get traction and get personal. *We* need to get traction and get personal. We need other people. We need to hear and take to heart other people's stories. We need God's creation. We need to understand our times. We need honesty about ourselves. We need fresh object lessons. We need embodied faith and love. We need many different wisdoms to illumine the different parts of life. The "Just . . ." formulas never meet the need.

A Recent Example

Consider briefly a "Just remember x" formula that has enjoyed particular popularity in recent years. Many preachers, teachers, counselors, and writers focus on the seventh item on our list. Past grace—justification by faith and adoption as God's child—has often been presented as the master key to Christian growth. The dynamic of the Christian life is portrayed as a matter of continually pressing into how God forgave and accepted you.[1] *You are sanctified by remembering and believing afresh that you are justified by what Jesus did on the cross for you.*

Is that true? Justification by faith in the sacrifice of Christ certainly is a cornerstone of our salvation. But is remembering that always the crucial ingredient in how we are progressively changed and sanctified? The Bible's answer to this pastoral and practical question is sometimes yes, often no. Consider this metaphor: Scripture portrays the transformation of our lives in a range of colors and shades. There are reds, yellows, and blues—with 16.8 million shades in between. So any monochromatic view of sanctification is like saying, "You are changed by the color red." For some Christians, some of the time, amid some life struggles, to remember the color red—justification by Christ's death, adoption as God's child, the forgiveness of sins—proves pivotal. For other Christians, at other times, facing other specific struggles, other colors prove pivotal.

How do we explain the dynamics of sanctification? How do forgiven sinners change? How do newborn saints learn to trust and love? What is the connecting link between what we say we believe and how we live? These are complex questions and have been controversial throughout Christian history. In exegetical and theological terms, the controversy asks, What is the relationship between

- justification and sanctification?
- law and gospel?
- indicatives (what Christ has done) and imperatives (how we are to live)?
- God's grace and God's commandments?
- receptive faith and active works?
- what the Spirit does and what you do?

These are different angles on the same very important, very practical question. Exegetical fidelity and theological clarity matter.

Though I claim no fresh answer to these questions, I have noticed two things about most discussions. First, most of them lack case studies. They do not reckon adequately with how *practical theology* operates—both in the Bible (which *is* practical theology in action) and in people's stories. When you look closely at people's lives, how do they actually change? Where do they get stuck? What does change—and what doesn't change? What is the process like? What are the typical ups and downs? How do you explain the advances and the regressions? How do we help each other? How does Scripture actually function in altering people's hearts and choices? How does trusting the God you need to trust connect to loving the people you need to love? What is the dynamic by which receiving grace becomes giving grace? How does the inworking hand and voice of the Spirit become expressed in the outworking of tangible fruit of the Spirit? And how do ministries of words, care, and action actually influence change in someone else?

Both Scripture and lives lived embody the answers to these practical theology questions. You can never actually capture the relationship between faith and works by lining up our theological categories in abstraction from these personal and practical questions. You need people to inhabit those categories—people who often don't neatly conform to the categories we use to explain something as inexplicable as life itself! You need stories.

Second, when we seek to express the debate in formal theological terms, all Christians agree in broad strokes. Three things precede any process of progressive transformation:

- God must initiate to reconcile our fatally broken relationship with him.
- Jesus Christ must accomplish his redeeming work for us.
- The Holy Spirit must change our sinful human nature.[2]

Yes and amen. We are saved from outside ourselves, and we are saved from ourselves. We are Christians. So, of course, justification and forgiveness (along with many other things) precede and undergird sanctification. Grace (which takes many forms) precedes and undergirds obedience. The Spirit (who does and says many things) precedes and undergirds our efforts. We have been saved. We are being saved. We work out our salvation.

And we will be saved. Every Christian also agrees—in broad strokes—that three kinds of things will culminate the process of transformation:

- Jesus Christ will finish his work by returning as King.
- The Spirit will perfect our human nature in love, joy, peace, and all other graces.
- We will know our Father face-to-face.

What God began and continues to do, he will finish. Progressive sanctification is about how we live in between God's laying the cornerstone and setting the capstone. As we have seen, grace operates in three tenses: past, present, and future. No one disagrees at this general level, because such generalizations are the rudiments of Christian faith.

But the burning question remains: *How* are disciples made along the way? This cannot be well understood either in the broad strokes of our theological agreement or in the refined nuances of theological disagreement. This is a practical theology question, a ministry question, a personal question, an interpersonal question. Could the primary key to our sanctification be to continually revisit how our broken relationship with God was reconciled by the work of Jesus? A vast Bible, centuries of pastoral experience, and innumerable testimonies bear joint witness that there is a lot more to it. When practical and pastoral implications are deduced from a sweeping theological generalization and then buttressed by selected texts and a single-stranded personal testimony, important things are overlooked.

When we look back into the stories and details of Scripture, and when we look out into the variety of life stories and pastoral experiences, we see a "manyness" that defies reductionism, a "pointedness" that defies tidy abstraction. That morning in January, Nan and I were changed by hearing the Lord say in essence, "I pursue my people in the desert, and I care for my beloved like an eagle with its nestlings." No doubt, many complementary doctrines explain, nuance, complement, fulfill, and abstract the words of Deuteronomy 32:10–12. The entirety of Christian faith operates in the deep structure, so we could justly say that "justification by faith in the death of Christ for our sins" deeply undergirds how this passage comes true. But if I had to pick a more immediate doctrinal underpinning, I'd point to "God's electing, pursuing love for his people," or perhaps "God's sovereign purposes working all things for good." Yet none of this doctrinal infrastructure was key to our sanctification moment on that day. Nan was helped by a vivid picture of personal care: she was found, encircled, cared for, and kept as the apple of God's eye. I was helped by a graphic metaphor: the Lord came down like an eagle, hovered over me, caught me up, and carried me on his wings.

3

TRUTH UNBALANCED
AND REBALANCED

What then is the relationship between theological infrastructure and how disciple making works? How does a graphic metaphor or a complex story relate to a doctrinal summary that seeks to faithfully capture its meaning? How can we think about progressive sanctification in a way that generates ministry traction? Here is a core premise: *Ministry "unbalances" truth for the sake of relevance; theology "rebalances" truth for the sake of comprehensiveness.*[1] Put another way, because you can only say one thing at a time, a timely word must be a selective word focusing on the need of the moment. And this selective focus produces a kind of imbalance. But stepping back from the need of the moment, many things can be said, and this larger theological picture helps us maintain balance. The whole truth is as wide as human experience, as deep as the human heart, and as unfathomable as the God who weighs all things and intervenes in all things.

The Art of Unbalancing

The first half of that premise might sound odd at first, but this is what it means. *The task in any ministry moment is to choose, emphasize, and "unbalance" truth for the sake of relevant application to particular persons and situations.* You can't say everything all at once—and you shouldn't try. The Bible's authors minister in this way. They say one relevant thing at a time. Deuteronomy 32:10–12 says one true thing in a particular way and leaves a thousand complementary truths unsaid. In experiential fact, Moses said one true thing in two particular ways, one of which became relevant to Nan, and the other of which became relevant to me! It was what we needed, and all we could take in at that moment.

This is how Jesus ministers. In the Gospels, he chooses to say and emphasize certain things, unbalancing the whole truth in order to say the relevant, timely word. When he talks with people, he is astonishingly concrete, direct, specific. He is not comprehensive or abstract. This is because the Gospels capture a series of ministry moments in which Jesus gives people what they need and can handle. By saying one thing, not everything, he is always challenging, always life-rearranging, always nourishing those who are listening.

Jesus's own example is one reason we know that "sanctification by remembering Christ's substitutionary death" cannot be the beating heart of all sanctification. Throughout the Gospels he is continually forming disciples by everything he does and says. His teaching ranges widely. The questions he asks probe from many angles, always teasing out what a person truly believes and is actually doing. Jesus sometimes reveals who he is and sometimes conceals who he is. He says yes to some requests and no to others.

And it is also important to remember that Christ's cross has multiple implications. His dying and death express a number of ways that Scripture is relevant to forming our faith and our obedience. Here are seven of the more obvious meanings—and I make no claim that these exhaustively explain a glory before which we bow.

First, consider how the cross reveals *the character of God*. Mercy meshes with justice. Steadfast love joins holy wrath. The "competing" sides of God's self-revelation demonstrate their perfect complementarity. God is light so bright that no man can dwell in his presence; God is love so tender that he makes his dwelling place with man. In other words, the cross is not just about us. Innumerable men and women have found this reality profoundly humbling, comforting, and sanctifying. Something incomprehensibly wonderful unfolds before our eyes. Fall on your knees, put your hand over your mouth, acknowledge your incomprehension, and worship. The cross says, "O come, let us adore him."

Second, consider how innumerable men and women have found *mercy, comfort, and joy* in what the cross accomplishes. It is most certainly about us. Jesus's death in our place means life, salvation, reconciliation with God, forgiveness, and hope. He died for us—weak, godless, sinful, his enemies. He made propitiation. He bore wrath. The Lamb of God made a substitutionary atonement. This is life-or-death relevant for every human being. Either Jesus saves your life, or you perish. Faith grasps Christ and lives. He justifies us by living the life we could never live, by dying the death we should have died, by being raised to the life that we shall share with him. The cross says, "I truly forgive you and accept you" (cf. Romans 1–11).

Third, consider how innumerable children of God find *strength in the reality that the powers of darkness and death were defeated* at the cross. Our enemies were disarmed. They were put to open shame. *Christus Victor* has triumphed in a drama of cosmic judgment and deliverance. His cross means crushing defeat for the Enemy, and the death of death, and the overcoming of lies, and the crucifying of sin. The cross says, "Don't be afraid. The ruler of this world is cast out" (cf. John 12:31; Col. 2:15).

Fourth, consider how countless men and women find *rest and comfort in the reality that Jesus sympathetically enters into suffering*. He not only identifies; he participates. He not only sympathizes; he feels it personally. He bears our griefs and sorrows as well as our sins. He does not treat lightly or pull back from the affliction of the afflicted. He hears their cry. The cross says, "You are not alone. I am with you. I understand. I hear you. I will help you in your time of need" (cf. Ps. 22:24; Heb. 4:16).

Fifth, consider that innumerable children of God find *encouragement in the friendship of Christ*. A man lays down his life for his friends—and Christ has befriended us. We were once his enemies, but he has won us over and won our hearts. The cross tangibly demonstrates how much God loves, and his love has a winsome effect. His love is more than a benevolent feeling of affection. He makes known his intimate counsel. He shows it by what he does. The cross says, "You are my friend. I open my heart to you and lay down my life for you" (cf. Ps. 25:14; John 15:15).

Sixth, consider that countless children of God find *strength, mercy, and hope in the Lord's Supper*. The cross creates a fellowship of common life together. The sweet cup of life that Jesus gives his disciples to drink is juxtaposed with the bitter cup of death from which he recoiled before willingly drinking. The living body of this Jesus nourishes us with the bread of life. The shed blood of this Jesus nourishes us with the wine of forgiveness. It says, "You are welcome here. Taste and see that the Lord is good. The banquet of life is coming" (cf. Matt. 26:26–29).

Seventh, consider how innumerable men and women gain *vision and encouragement from* how *Jesus died*. The seven things he said while he was pinned to the cross are pointedly relevant to how you and I live and die:

- "Father, forgive them, for they know not what they do" (Luke 23:34).
- "Truly, I say to you, today you will be with me in Paradise" (Luke 23:43).
- "He said to his mother, 'Woman, behold, your son!' Then he said to the disciple, 'Behold, your mother!'" (John 19:26–27).
- "My God, my God, why have you forsaken me?" (Matt. 27:46).
- "I thirst" (John 19:28).
- "It is finished" (John 19:30).

- "Father, into your hands I commit my spirit!"
  (Luke 23:46).

Jesus's first three words reach with mercy to others. His last four words reach out in need for his Father. Why is this significant? Jesus's actual first-person experience expresses the fundamental extroversions of candid faith and personalized love. We can easily imagine how being tortured to death and facing imminent asphyxiation would pull any one of us into a whirlpool of self-absorption in pain and vulnerability. A person in such agony reacts in typical ways: despair, impotent rage, self-pity, terror, and an overpowering urge to numb or escape pain. But amid intense suffering, Jesus cries out to the Father and cares for the people around him. We watch and hear how honestly he lives the Psalms. We witness how specifically he lives out the commandments to love his God and his neighbors. We stand in awe.

We learn from our Savior's way of dying something important about what it means to be his disciples. The way our Master did his dying sets an exemplary pattern for discipleship into his image. He calls us to follow him, walking the *via crucis*. I have had the privilege of knowing wise Christians who were trusting, caring, thoughtful, and hopeful in the way they lived. And even as they were hurting and dying, even when greatly compromised by illness, they retained the essence of those qualities. I've seen the image of Jesus remade in friends who expressed faith and gratitude even while facing the last enemy. Jesus gave them a way of life. He gives you a way of life. He gives me a way of life. He is sanctifying us into this image of faith and love amid whatever troubles we face. The cross says, "Follow me."

The Son of God reveals God's perfect love and perfect justice before our eyes. The Sin-Bearer brings mercies and righteousness from God. The triumphant King slays all the dragons. The true companion enters sympathetically into our afflictions. The friend lays down his life for us. The host welcomes us to his banquet table. The role model walks ahead of us on the difficult path of faith and love.

You will find it hard to take in all of these at the same time. Each one matters profoundly. Each of these meanings of the cross changes our lives. Each of these realities has a sanctifying effect. Each disciples us into the humility, confidence, kindness, and hope that adorn Christian faith with its true loveliness. Each is relevant in a different way. Must we choose? Must one exclude the others or relegate the others to the shadows? Which of these is most relevant to you in your current situation?

You will find it hard to talk with another person about all of these at once. If you try, you will likely overwhelm your struggling friend with too much truth at one time. You will miss the pertinent need of the moment. Which is most timely to this person in this situation facing these struggles? And will all these meanings live in your heart so they can be expressed with your lips when the need of the moment calls?

In order to live well yourself and minister well to others, you will want to learn the art of skillful unbalancing. But even in the way I have been discussing the art of unbalancing, I have sought to avoid becoming unbalanced. By noting how each of the varied meanings of "the cross" might become salient and relevant, we have already seen the importance of rebalancing.

The Art of Rebalancing

Practical ministry focuses on one truth out of many for the sake of relevance to particular settings and needs. But the second half of our core premise is equally important. *The task of theological reflection is to "rebalance" truth for the sake of comprehensiveness.* It helps to know all you can that might need saying, even while knowing you can say only one thing at a time.

Balance has two aspects. The first rebalancing is achieved by faithfully abstracting and generalizing. It is extremely helpful for us to understand our Christian faith topically. So *systematic theology* serves us well by organizing revelation into logical categories. When done well, it also demonstrates the dynamic, organic interrelationship between complementary truths. (It often does better with the logical categories than with illustrating the organic linkages between doctrines.) And it is equally helpful for us to understand our Christian faith as an unfolding story of redemption. *Biblical theology* serves us well by tracing the sequence of God's actions and words through history. When done well, it also shows how the big story is composed of numerous scenes, incidents, moments, snapshots. (It often does better at sketching the metanarrative than at maintaining contact with the micronarratives.) Generalization helps us to maintain a vision for the whole. A comprehensive theological vision protects us from exaggerating, ignoring, or overgeneralizing.

A second kind of rebalancing is achieved by wide-ranging knowledge of the Bible. Scripture embodies the organic interrelationship of many truths. Scripture unfolds the drama of redemption in many small moments. And Scripture addresses the many different facets of human experience. For example, here are three pairs of passages that demonstrate how attending to the scope of Scripture brings the flexibility of wisdom to how you engage and communicate with others:

- The major question animating both the Psalms and 1 Peter is how to face experiences of suffering. But the Psalms delve more deeply into the sufferer's relationship with God, while Peter delves more into the sufferer's relationships with people.
- In contrast, both Proverbs and 2 Peter are animated by the need to distinguish false voices from true voices, and a dead-end lifestyle from a fruitful way of life. But Proverbs focuses more on the treacheries of daily life, while Peter focuses on the treachery of authoritative false teachers.
- In John 11:21, 32, after the death of Lazarus, first Martha and then Mary approached Jesus, each saying, "Lord, if you had been here, my brother would not have died." He replied with a theological lesson for Martha and for his fatalistic disciples. But with Mary and the skeptical onlookers, Jesus's response was deep emotion followed by dramatic action.

Different existential questions call for different ministry approaches. The breadth of Scripture shows in case after case how different ministry contexts generate different messages and actions. Sensitivity to the variety protects us from exaggerating, ignoring, and overgeneralizing.

In order to actually minister to people, you need wise selectivity, while bearing in mind the fullest possible repertoire of options from which to choose. You do not build a house with only one tool in your toolbox when God gives you a truckload of tools. But you do use your tools one at a time, the right tool for the right job.

The unbalance-rebalance dynamic is crucial for how we grow and for how we help others. Understanding this also helps to explain why "balanced" teaching often seems general, nonspecific, and even dull, while "unbalanced" application sounds pointed, relevant, and scintillating. Teaching that is only balanced is, in this sense, pointless. It discusses topics rather than touching people on matters of urgent concern. Ministry electrifies when it connects something to someone rather than trying to say everything to no one in particular. Theologians and teachers, beware!

The delicate relationship between the whole truth that orients and particular truths that scintillate also helps explain how "unbalanced" teaching can go bad. There are good reasons why not every Christian is impressed with the one truth that may have revolutionized your life. That one partial truth may have really helped you, and it may be drawing a particular kind of person to your ministry. But when one truth morphs into The Truth—the whole truth—it becomes an ax to grind. It promises a panacea, a "cure all." As this happens, it slides in the direction of a magic formula, a "secret" to be discovered, not the plain, simple wisdom of God. A word that really helps some kinds of people can prove unhelpful—even misleading and destructive— to people who need one of the other kinds of help that God gives. Preachers and counselors, beware!

Am I saying, for example, that pointing a person back to the justification of sinners could actually be pastorally hurtful? Yes. If what you need to know is "I am with you right now. I am your refuge in this affliction," then you may well go hungry if you are given "I died for your sins once and for all." You might beat up on yourself for your lack of faith, or you might go cold to God because a message that claimed it would help you doesn't seem to touch your need for help. In the long run, a single truth harped on will disappoint even its devotees. In another season of life, facing a different struggle, they too will need the other kinds of help. What once sizzled becomes boring, a repetitive pat answer that no longer delivers.

The story with which I opened this book was "unbalanced." On that particular day, Nan and I stumbled into God's presence with low expectations and only a reading plan that told us to open the Bible to a particular place. The Lord surprised us with evocative promises and ignited faith's imagination. We obeyed in practical ways because our imaginations caught fire. That morning we were sanctified by overarching promises that prompted actions.

But is that how it always works?

4

GOD MEETS US WITH
HIS COMMANDS

I am now writing three days after God used the promises of Deuteronomy 32 to refresh Nan and me. These past three days have been marked by an entirely different dynamic. Each morning I've been sanctified by intentionally taking specific *commands* to heart. One familiar sentence has been my daily companion in the Holy Spirit's discipling work: "The aim of our charge is love that issues from a pure heart and a good conscience and a sincere faith" (1 Tim. 1:5). Here Paul describes the goal of all ministry. Mature faith and wise love are what holiness looks like. This is the sanctification that discipleship produces.

Love for God and Neighbor Is *Good*
This transformation of both behavior and motive is entirely rooted in sure promises of ongoing blessing: "Grace, mercy, and

peace from God the Father and Christ Jesus our Lord" (1 Tim. 1:2). But taken for what it actually says, Paul's charge is law in the best and foundational sense of the word. Law is good. God's moral law describes faith and love. "Trust in the LORD with all your heart" (Prov. 3:5) is a call for a pure heart, a good conscience, and a sincere faith. "Look . . . to the interests of others" (Phil. 2:4) is a call for genuine love. What God commands expresses Jesus's intimate purpose in working with us to set us free.

The moral law is not only a standard against which sinners fail, driving us to need our Savior. God is love, and his law reveals both the image in which he created us and the image into which he is recreating us. Law describes loving well. It is not cold, legalistic, threatening, and impersonal. It is warm, humane, desirable, personal. God's law describes how full humanness operates when walking free. It pictures how wisdom perceives and acts. It casts a vision for what we are becoming under the gentle, firm hand of our Savior's grace. Why has this law of Christ proved so nourishing to me and had such a noticeable impact during these past three days?

Here is a bit of backstory that captures how this rich command has been touching my life. For starters, I am not a morning person—cobwebs are an understatement. I laugh aloud when I read the description of the contrast between two of my favorite literary characters, Stephen Maturin and Jack Aubrey: "Stephen was still stupid from heavy sleep. . . . He was a frowzy, unwashed object, his wits not yet gathered into an orderly troop, whereas Jack was in the full tide of daily life."[1] I can identify with that frowzy stupidity, that mind adrift in a disorderly maze. I can identify with that contrast between my slow start and certain friends who arise buoyantly awake and girded for action at 5:30 each morning. But God does not leave me frowzy. In each of the past three mornings, as I have consciously reflected on God's will for me expressed in 1 Timothy 1:5, that disorderly troop has gradually fallen into line and marched into the day on a rising tide of gladness and purpose.

Paul charges me to consider others because I am awake to God. Holiness in my relationships with others is the bottom line. Sanctification means pointedly, freely, genuinely loving other people. Lord, help me to stop, to care, to notice, to listen, to express candid appreciation, to share my life. And he helps. This goal has marked my conscious intentions when I've participated in meetings, when I've chatted with coworkers in the hallway, when I've conversed in face-to-face counseling, when I've come home to Nan. These words have helped me to treat others well. Being indifferent, or opinionated, or avoidant, or preoccupied comes easy. But it is a bit of holiness when I am happy to see someone, when I ask a question and mean it, when I listen attentively, when I genuinely affirm, when I push back candidly and constructively. These words from Paul's letter have marked my reflections on this topic. Father, help me to write constructively, according to your people's need of the moment. May these words give grace.

Loving other people comes from somewhere: "a pure heart and a good conscience and a sincere faith." Caring for others (horizontal sanctification) arises from reorientation to God (vertical sanctification). I have been consciously reflecting and seeking the three ways this command describes our reorientation to God:

- *A pure heart.* Father, make me less divided by competing loyalties and agendas, by unruly desires and anxieties. Make me love you more simply.
- *A good conscience.* Lord, attune my conscience so that I weigh all things the way you weigh them. Make my conscience alive and active. Imbue my conscience with Christ's merciful, redeeming purposes.
- *A sincere faith.* Holy Spirit, make me simple, candid, and resilient. Make me trust you in need, in gratitude, in joy, in dependence.

When we ask anything according to his will, he hears us and we will be sanctified.

Awaken to the Good Ways God Works

In the past week, on one day Nan and I were surprised by gifts of sheer promise that address the experience of feeling harassed, overwhelmed, and alone. The Spirit's sanctifying word came as a pungently evocative Old Testament metaphor, as an indicative, as gospel (in the large sense of the word), as a gift of grace feeding faith. The obedience that followed arose spontaneously, uncalled for within the passage itself.

Then on other days the Spirit's sanctifying word came as I intentionally pondered a command. I fed on imperatives. The imperatives portray what Jesus is like. This law of Christ and law of love guided my intercession, my aspiration, and my efforts. This apostolic word called me to the energetic obedience of faith and the energetic obedience of love—premised on, dependent on, and seeking the grace, mercy, and peace of God and Christ.

The work of Christ on the cross—so foundational theologically—was entirely *implicit* throughout this particular week, neither mentioned in these Scriptures nor said aloud or consciously pondered. It was not absent—the foundation of a house is always foundational. When there are cracks in the foundation, when the house is sagging, you work directly on the foundation. But other times you simply live in a well-furnished house.

Throughout my Christian life, there have been—and I trust there will be—many other words that prove life-rearranging, day-rearranging, and moment-rearranging. (And remember, here we are only discussing the Word-and-Spirit aspect of sanctification. Many other things affect our sanctification—the input and example of other people, participation in worship and sacrament, noticing God's creation, experiencing how he works within suffering, learning candid prayer, and so forth.)

Neither of my two specific examples from this past week touches everyone or every situation. Consider other human needs that cry out for a Redeemer. What speaks to a deceitful serial adulterer? To a child transfixed by the beauty of falling snow? To a woman facing a diagnosis of metastasized ovarian cancer? To a repentant adulterer torn by guilt? To a businesswoman facing an ethical dilemma in her workplace? To a newly married, virginal couple about to have sexual relations for the first time? To a depressed elderly man for whom the spark of life went out twenty years ago when his wife died? And even that list names only a few categories of persons—and individuals are individuals, not categories. What will be the timely word for me tomorrow morning? For you? For the next person you talk with?

Ministry, Scripture, and the Spirit speak variously, so be careful how you generalize about sanctification This is also why any two wise, godly friends will speak differently into your life, even when addressing the same situation. Organic unity (balance) and infinite adaptability (unbalance) characterize the wisdom that sanctifies us. There is no formula or pat answer. When two friends say the same thing, or when you say the same thing to every struggler, it is probably a pat answer.

My stories provide several core samples of the pastoral application of Scripture unto sanctification. But what if I attempted to draw theological conclusions from my experience? In the first case, I might conclude and teach, "All you need are the wide-ranging promises of God. Simply trust God's initiating and intervening care. Obedience will flow spontaneously. Any effort and struggle in the Christian life is the struggle to remember that God watches over those he loves." But if I formed my theology from the second case, I might conclude and teach, "God's grace lays the foundation once for all. Now focus all your efforts on loving God and neighbor. Think hard. Plan well. Make every effort to discipline yourself in practical obedience." In either case, I would have extrapolated a plausible but inadequate generalization from a lovely truth and an experience that is personally significant. Each formulation almost works. But inexorably, the first generalization drifts toward pietism, and the second generalization drifts toward moralism.

In the long run, each of those overgeneralizations creates both theological problems and pastoral problems. Neither generalization teaches you how Christ reproves a high-handed evildoer. Neither speaks comfort to a person in anguish, who needs to know that God is a safe place. Neither directly addresses those who are weary, who need faith that one day this struggle with sin and sorrow will end, who need to know that all things will be made new. Neither reminds you that Jesus Christ saves even the chief of sinners.

5

WE ARE SANCTIFIED
BY REMEMBERING
OUR JUSTIFICATION

Scripture does not tell us "the secret things" that "belong to the LORD" (Deut. 29:29) but speaks the open things that God intends to reshape our lives. One catalyst for this book was the prevalence of "Just remember the cross" teachings about sanctification. But I don't want you to get the wrong idea. I do want you to remember that God accepts you because of who Jesus Christ is and what he has done. Our efforts at making ourselves acceptable or doing penance for our failings are not why he makes us his own. I've critiqued an overstated message, but there is life-saving good in the message rightly stated.

Clear Statement, Not Overstatement

Here are some of the catchphrases that claim to describe the essential dynamic of sanctification: "meditate on your justification"; "remember the gospel"; "contemplate the cross"; "preach the gospel to yourself"; "realize you are accepted by Christ's performance, not yours." Each of these exhortations can be applied in a way that is very helpful. But when *timely* "unbalancing" becomes *repetitively* and *assertively* unbalanced, these phrases can become misleading both pastorally and personally. Other helpful, needful things get drowned out. Standing alone, these statements lead to the following generalizations:

- Sanctification essentially involves the activity of remembering, believing, and resting on justification. Rehearsal of Jesus's substitutionary death for your sins is the key dynamic driving our sanctification.
- Self-salvation through our efforts is the sin of sins. The attempt at self-justification through performance is the deepest, most persistent, and most significant problem hindering and necessitating sanctification.
- When the Bible says to "make every effort," the struggle of the Christian life is about the work of remembering that we are justified and accepted by what Christ has done. Sanctification is not about our behavior, but about clinging to Christ's mercy.

These generalizations are simply not true. The Bible explicitly shows and tells something different. People's stories show and tell something different. As selective, pastoral applications in certain cases and situations, all of these statements contain something true and helpful. Yet, stated as theological generalizations about the universal dynamics of the Christian life, they are overstated and reductionistic. Overstatement always underdelivers in the long run. Reductionism promises too much with too little. When theory trumps reality, reality will bite back.

But when our theory and practice comport with reality, reality gets reshaped. You grow as wise and flexible as the Scriptures, which have a knack for adapting to the messy complexities and idiosyncrasies of reality. Scripture will boldly speak one unbalanced bit of relevant truth into a situation where appropriate, and then in the next paragraph speak in an entirely different way to a different situation. If we restate the three earlier overstatements more modestly—each as one possible pastoral directive among many potentially helpful pastoral words—the profound truths in them clearly emerge:

- *Sometimes* you are sanctified by pointedly remembering that God justifies you on the basis of Christ's righteousness, atoning sacrifice, and resurrection.
- Basing your relationship with God on your performance is *one common problem* that both calls for sanctification and hinders sanctification.
- *Sometimes* it is a struggle to remember that you are justified by Christ's work—and it is worth struggling to get that foundation clear.

Do you see how this list differs from the previous one? Plain, simple, accurate understatements have a way of delivering more than you expect in the long run. You can honestly ask yourself, "Does this describe me or not?" Your honest answer will be either yes or no.

Remember Your Justification

Let's zero in on the times when the answer is yes. Are we changed by knowing that we are justified by faith? Yes and amen. To consciously remember and take to heart that you are fully accepted by God because of what Jesus Christ has done for you makes a big difference in your Christian life. He reached out to take you by the hand and saved you. In friendship, preaching, counseling, and discipleship, this may be *exactly* the message that needs to be featured. This truth is theologically foundational to being a Christian, to being forgiven, to being made right with God, to having the courage to be candid about our sins (one of the foundational transformations of the sanctification process). It is elementary—not in the modern sense of being as easy as ABC, but in the old sense of being basic, fundamental, essential, constitutive.

Consciousness of this truth not only works to change people at the inception of Christian faith. The New Testament letters are written to Christians. As an aspect of apostolic pastoral care unto sanctification, they often remind God's people of what Christ did for us. It is no surprise that I have known many true Christians who only gradually came to understand the significance of what Christ did on the cross. Growing in such knowledge has been a crucial part of their sanctification, their growing assurance and confidence, their understanding of sinfulness, their gratitude. Growth in those things is often slow and hard-won.

What are some ways that consciously grasping and resting upon justification by faith directly ministers pastorally? This truth often powerfully affects people who are oriented toward their own performance. It comforts those disturbed by the sting of their failures. It disturbs those who are comfortable and self-satisfied in their successes. Anxiety and depression might seem like the opposite of pride and self-confidence, but they can originate in the same underlying compulsion.

Justification by faith is comforting. Men and women who doubt that they are acceptable and accepted, who struggle with believing that God could ever love them, who feel that they always fall short, or who slink in shame around God are foundationally helped. Listen, learn, and trust that God willingly and truly reconciles us to himself through Christ. He raises up those crushed by failure, self-condemnation, guilt, and shame. His mercies touch our need.

Justification by faith is also disturbing. Men and women who are overly self-confident; who try to prove themselves to God, others, and themselves by their goodness; who try to save the world by their efforts; or who busy themselves building a résumé and crafting an identity are humbled. God humbles those who are proud, self-confident, and self-righteous. He teaches us to need his mercies.

If God Is for Us . . .

So whether you think you are too bad or think you are good enough, it makes a difference to know that we become right with God by faith in Christ and what he has done. Such faith is an empty hand reaching to receive life. Here is one biblical description of how he has done it:

> If God is for us, who can be against us? He who did not spare his own Son but gave him up for us all, how will he not also with him graciously give us all things? Who shall

bring any charge against God's elect? It is God who justifies. Who is to condemn? Christ Jesus is the one who died—more than that, who was raised—who is at the right hand of God, who indeed is interceding for us. (Rom. 8:31–34)

Take this to heart. Don't ever forget. If you feel *un*worthy and yet all these things are true, then the door to the Father stands wide open. If you think you are worthy, then because these things are true, this is the only door to the Father. He means it when he says, "Come to me." So whatever your struggle, take him at his word.

So far so good. But now notice something significant about the pastoral purpose of Romans 8:18–39. Paul openly states his reasons for mentioning God's justifying mercies in 8:31–34. He is not even thinking about performance-oriented people. Self-salvation efforts, our sins, and placing personal faith in Christ's atoning work for forgiveness are not in view.[1] The direct application in *this* discussion of justification serves people who face hardship, weakness, and hostility. They are tempted to doubt God's love, to feel abandoned by God, to feel threatened by "the sufferings of this present time" (8:18). Romans 8:31–34 mentions that God has already justified us by Christ's death as one way to give hope and comfort to sufferers, not to remind anxious sinners or obsessive strivers. The original takeaway was not "You can get off that performance treadmill—God does not condemn you for your sins." The takeaway was "However hard life gets, nothing and no one has power to destroy you and separate you from the love of God." The second half of Romans 8 sanctifies you when earthly life is a vale of weakness, affliction, groaning, and tears.

In the pastoral context of Romans 8, justification by faith serves as one subpoint in a long chain of subpoints aiming to make a far larger point: *God is for you*. One way he shows that he is for you is that he justifies sinners. And that is one of a cascade of ways that God demonstrates his essential attitude toward you. I will not unpack the dozen or more ways that Romans 8:18–39 expresses and reinforces the Lord's "I am for you." But notice how, just within Romans 8:31–34, the assurance that God is your justifier joins hands with four other ways he shows how he loves you:

- God did not spare his very own Son. This is not repeating how and why forgiveness and justification were accomplished. Paul is describing the attitude and purpose that animated God to give us his nearest, dearest, and best. *He was for you.*
- God chose us to be his own by his electing, possessive love. This points out that God freely sets his affection on his chosen people. *He was for you all along.*
- If God has already given us his own Son, then of course he will freely give us every other good thing. This points to many other blessings, past, present, and future, that come in train with Christ (many of which are mentioned earlier in Romans 8). *He is abundantly for you.*
- This Christ Jesus, who died and was raised to life, continues to intercede on our behalf. This points to the living Christ and what he is doing right now. *He is still for you.*

God does not condemn us but loves us—and he is the one who decides. Many interlocking, mutually reinforcing, soul-nourishing truths serve a larger promise. In the midst of painful circumstances, don't lose heart, because *every* blessing (including justification) works unto your sanctification, your faith, your obedience, and your hope.

And there is more, of course. Romans 8:35–39 plunges into the morass of distress and trouble that we face—including death. It points out all the powerful forces arrayed against us. Can anything separate us from the love of Christ? Nothing can separate us from the love of God in Christ Jesus our Lord. He will be *for* you forever, and then he will be *with* you forever.

6

WHAT CHANGES YOU?

One goal of this book is to connect the details that make us different from each other with the themes that make us similar. Though God's ways with us follow no one formula, the variety in life and in Scripture is not random and chaotic. It organizes into certain patterns. It contains certain kinds of ingredients. No single factor, no one truth, no protocol can capture how and why a person grows into Christ's image. Multiple factors always cooperate in progressive sanctification. But God does help us keep our bearings amid a multitude of variables. This chapter will give a simple framework to encompass the variables in how God works to change us.

Keeping It Simple

Human beings do well with simple. We do poorly with complicated. And we do poorly with simplistic. True wisdom has a delightful simplicity. Foolishness either overcomplicates or oversimplifies. Two of my favorite modern proverbs comment on the relationship between the simplistic, the complicated, and the truly simple.[1]

> I would not give a fig for the simplicity this side of complexity, but I would give my life for the simplicity on the other side of complexity.

> On the near side of complexity is simplistic; on the far side of complexity is simple.

The truly simple accounts for all complexities.

For example, consider Jesus's words, "You cannot serve God and money" (Matt. 6:24; Luke 16:13). That's simple. What do you live for? Whether you inherited millions, or work hard to make a decent living, or live in deep poverty on the margin between life and death, Jesus's words search you out. Do your money sins cluster around anxiety? Conspicuous consumption? Coveting? Stealing? Presumptuous confidence? Despair? Jesus's simple truth accounts for you, no matter what your economic status, cultural background, or personal quirks. Simple words probe and account for every complexity. That is the sort of generalization that serves us well. It is not reductionistic. It is not vague. It does useful work in helping us understand ourselves and each other.

How do we understand the relationship between simple and complex without becoming simplistic and reductionistic? How do we understand the relationship between simple and complex without getting lost in endless complications, permutations, and variations? What changes you for the better? What turns your life around?

- Does God turn you from darkness to light?
- Does Scripture turn you from lies to truth?
- Do wise people turn you from foolishness to wisdom?
- Do challenging life circumstances turn you from vanities to enduring good?
- Do you yourself turn to God and turn away from world, flesh, and Devil?

Yes. All of the above. Though the details bring innumerable variables to the table, constructive change occurs through the interplay of these five factors: God, Scripture, other people, life circumstances, and the human heart. Figure 1 is a simple picture that captures these five cooperating elements.

Figure 1. Five factors of sanctification

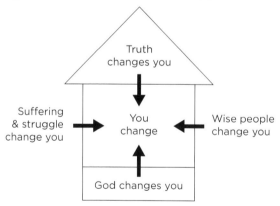

The way any life unfolds is nonformulaic, yet variants on these five factors intertwine within every story of our discipleship. This interplay appears everywhere in Scripture. The story of your life in Christ is composed of these elements. Let's take a brief look at each one.

Keeping Five Factors in View

First, and foundational to all, *God himself changes you.* "It is God who works in you, both to will and to work for his good pleasure" (Phil. 2:13). He intervenes in your life, turning you from suicidal self-will to the kingdom of life. He raises you in Christ when you are dead in trespasses and sins. He restores hearing when you are deaf (you could not hear him otherwise). He gives sight when you are blind (you could not see him otherwise). He is immediately and personally present, a life-creating voice, a strong and strengthening hand. All good fruit in our lives comes by the Holy Spirit's working on scene. Jesus said it was better if he went away, because the Holy Spirit would come (John 16:7). The Holy Spirit continues to do the things that Jesus does—continually adding to the number of books that could be written. The stories I've told thus far are not just about what has happened to me and what I've done. They are about what Jesus Christ has done as he goes about saving and sanctifying me through all my days.

Second, *the Word of truth changes you.*

> The testimony of the LORD is sure,
> making wise the simple. (Ps. 19:7)

God communicates messages to us—many messages. Scripture speaks with a true voice into a world churning with false voices. Scripture reveals innumerable features of God's person, purposes, will, promises, and actions. Scripture clarifies every facet of human experience. I come to know myself truly as I live before the eyes of the One whose opinion matters. It is no accident that Scripture appears in each of the stories I have told.

Of course Scripture and God work in harmony. In fact, all five dimensions are complementary—and all ultimately depend on the hand of God. One lovely expression of the interplay between the Word of God and the God of the Word occurs in Romans 15. Paul first points out how *Scripture* changes us: "Whatever was written in former days was written for our instruction, that through endurance and through the encouragement of the Scriptures we might have hope" (Rom. 15:3). A few sentences later, Paul asks God himself to change us, to give us the very things that his Word calls for and calls forth: "May the God of hope fill you with all joy and peace in believing, so that by the power of the Holy Spirit you may abound in hope" (Rom. 15:13). In Scripture, God comes in person. We participate by hearing and responding.[2]

Third, *wise people change you.* "Whoever walks with the wise becomes wise" (Prov. 13:20). Godly growth is most frequently mediated through the gifts and graces of brothers and sisters in Christ. At the most basic corporate level, you can't call on God unless you believe in him; you can't believe in him unless you hear of him; you can't hear of him unless someone proclaims him (Rom. 10:14). Good worship, preaching, teaching, prayer, and sacraments have radiant, fruitful effects. Similarly, the honesty and graciousness, humility and clarity, good sense and convictions of others have radiant, fruitful effects (James 3:17–18). Good role models make a huge difference (2 Tim. 3:10–11). It is a great mercy to know people who deal gently with your ignorance and waywardness, because they know their own weakness and sinfulness, and they know the mercies of Christ (Heb. 5:2–3). It makes a huge difference when other people are able to comfort you in your afflictions, because God is bringing comfort into their afflictions (2 Cor. 1:4).[3]

Fourth, *suffering, struggle, and troubles change you.* "Although he was a son, he learned obedience through what he suffered" (Heb. 5:8). God works on us in the midst of trouble because trouble catches our attention. Difficulties make us need him. Faith has to sink roots, as profession deepens into reality. Martin Luther called *tentatio*—affliction, trial, difficulty, struggle—the "touchstone" of Christian experience. He said that hardships were his greatest teacher because they made Scripture and prayer come alive. The difficulties that we experience necessitate grace by awakening a true sense of weakness and need. This is where the Spirit is working. People change because something is hard, not because everything goes well; something—including myself—is off. Ministry traffics in trouble because Christ enters trouble, lives through trouble, is unafraid of trouble, speaks and acts into trouble. Struggles force us to need God. And we learn to love the way Christ loves only by experiencing the hard things that he experienced in loving us.[4]

The darkness of the human condition is characterized by two immense wrongs that create turmoil throughout our lives: a complex mix of moral evils arises from inside us; a complex mix of situational evils besets us. The Bible uses the word *evil* to describe both sin and suffering, just as we do in English. Something *inside* us is wrong. People believe, think, feel, want, and do bad things. Of course, the obvious atrocities are moral evils. But the falsity, self-deception, and godlessness of "normal" life and the misshapenness of "normal" desires similarly count as moral evil in God's assessment. We are "off," in relation to both God and other people. And things *outside* us are wrong. Bad things happen to us. Other people betray us. We face losses, sicknesses, and death. We swim in the falsehoods of our sociocultural milieu. A Liar and Murderer is out to deceive and kill us. In sum, we face troubles (externally); we are troublesome (interpersonally); and we are troubled (psychologically), struggling both with what we face and with who we are.

Fifth, *you change*. "You turned to God from idols to serve the living and true God" (1 Thess. 1:9). We turn—from darkness to light, from false gods to the only true God, from death to life, from unbelief to faith. You ask for help because you need help. You repent. You believe, trust, seek, take refuge. You are honest. You remember, listen, obey, fear, hope, love, give thanks, weep, confess, praise, delight, walk. Notice all these active verbs; they speak of wholehearted, whole-person action. These are the fruitful characteristics of a flourishing life. No one does any of this for you. You are not passive. You are not a puppet or a robot. You are 100 percent responsible, and yet you are 100 percent dependent on outside help. Any other way of putting it makes you either far too independent or far too passive. Notice, too, that none of these active verbs is a one-and-done. These are a way of life.

Keeping the Five Factors Together

Each factor contributes to how we change. They are present in differing degrees as our lives are rescripted. The greater part of wisdom consists in understanding the *relationship between* complementary truths. Wisdom involves having a feel for how each of these factors comes into play in relation to the others.

There is a rough theological order to how I have presented them, captured to some degree by the visual metaphor of a house (fig. 1, p. 63). They begin with God himself as foundational, and then with his overarching Word. Then comes the influence of other people. These three are the most obvious agencies of grace. I've then located us within the stress of the hardships and failures that catch our attention. Finally, you are the one who lives in the house, the person who changes direction. Grace comes to fruition in a change of mind—in turning, hoping, taking refuge, trusting, loving, and obeying. But this logical order is not always the way life happens.

In ministry to others (as in our own lives), we encounter the unpredictability of human experience. Any of these dimensions can arrive front and center in awareness. Often some suffering or personal failure initially catches a person's attention. Something troubles you. Perhaps you experience loss, betrayal, disappointment, futility—"any affliction" (2 Cor. 1:4) or "trials of various kinds" (James 1:2). Perhaps you struggle with guilt over a past sin or a present pattern of sinning—ill temper, immoralities, lying, complaining, an eating disorder, an abortion, selfishness, gluttony, worry, willfulness, or any of a thousand other defections. Usually hardships and sins come tangled together.

Other people always matter. Often a friend—perhaps even a stranger—shows himself or herself to be significantly caring and admirably wise. Often some church community communicates in Word and worship, in actions and attitudes, something attractive and right. The more you grow, the more you realize how other people and the gathered church matter.

In some way or other, a biblical passage—something true—

catches your attention as inescapably relevant. The more you grow, the more Scripture appears early in the process. You come to orient yourself by Scripture. By learning to listen, you learn to identify sin and suffering more accurately. You learn the kinds of people to rely on. You learn Jesus. As you take Scripture to heart, you become like a tree planted by streams of water, bearing fruit in season.

And, by definition, a person who changes takes action. You do something. You believe something. You ask for help, from a friend, from God, from both. You make different choices. You change your mind, your attitudes, your feelings, your goal in life, the way you treat others, your habits.

And you find, sooner or later, that God himself has been working all along—within the hardships, amid the sins, by the friendships, through his Word, in you. The farther you walk on this road, the more you realize that God is the decisive actor and foundational factor in the drama.

This is how sanctification works. Your entire Christian life is a series of variations and permutations of this five-dimensional process. This is how you grow. This is how you live. This is how you minister to others, loving them well in their need. This is how you arrive in heaven, seeing Jesus face-to-face, and finding that you have been made like him.

7

MY STORY (1)

We began this book by considering the last lines of John's Gospel and all the other books that might be written about what Jesus has done. We have consolidated our thinking by identifying the factors that come into play as we change. Now let's look at some of those other stories in this and the following chapters.

Of all the possible books telling what Jesus does, the book I know best is the one I am living. What I will say of my experience is necessarily and intentionally idiosyncratic—yet there are common themes that no doubt will resonate with readers. I think you will find both the idiosyncrasy and the commonality helpful. It is freeing to realize that your life, like mine, does not happen in boilerplate. You and I are not clones of anyone else. Every particular of your story will be different from mine—yet at the thematic level there are deep continuities between us. The kinds of things I struggle with are analogous to the kinds of things you struggle with. The ways Jesus meets me are analogous to the ways he meets you. Analogous, but not identical. God seems to love variety. You and I do not reduce to a category. Our Father is raising children, and every child I've ever known is unique. You cannot live someone else's story.

In this chapter and the next I will tell stories that have been touchpoints in my own Christian experience. In each story you will notice how all five factors are present and operating to bring change for the good. Each story has a somewhat different quality. Different situational variables come into play. Different personal issues are at stake. God intervenes in different ways. Different truths prove salient. Different people help in a variety of ways.

August 31, 1975

I came to Christian faith when I was twenty-five years old. My conversion was dramatic. In high school I had become preoccupied with existential questions: What lasts? What matters? What is meaningful? Who am I? Four lines of development gave force and shape to the questions and answers.

First, in my teens I became entirely estranged from the nominal, mainline version of churchgoing in which I had been raised. I never heard that Jesus Christ was anything more than a moral example of a man who did a lot of good. Christianity, as I experienced it, seemed like a polite veneer for people who didn't want to face hard realities.

Second, during those same years, I was immediately confronted with death and depravity: bullying (of me and others), the murder of a classmate, suicidal friends, exposure to pornography, people self-immolating on drugs. I was a passenger in a car that killed a man as he walked down a dark country road. I can still see his face—he turned toward our headlights in the last seconds, and I looked into his eyes as we hit him.

And I sat at my grandfather's bedside after he had a serious stroke. He was rummaging through his achievements, relationships, aspirations, and travels. He was searching for something that retained meaning, something he could hold on to, something that he could tell me mattered in life. But everything he mentioned seemed to crumble before his eyes as he spoke. In the end, all he could say was that life is more than money, and all he could do was break down and weep. After saying goodbye, I sat on the steps outside the hospital and wept too.

And then there were the normal disillusionments in the years during and after college. Neither academics, nor athletics, nor career could bear the weight of identity and meaning. Close relationships failed. A foray into drug use almost unhinged me. Awareness of my own egocentrism was slowly dawning. We're always the last to know the person in the mirror.

Third, I matriculated into Harvard as a math and science major, but I soon migrated to psychology and social sciences, and then moved on to literature and the arts. The hard sciences scratch the fringe of big questions. The social sciences dig deeper into human affairs, but though they describe some of what goes on, they can never say what it all means. The arts and humanities take a deeper look at the questions that really matter: life and death, love and hate, truth and falsity, desire and loss, good and evil. Through reading Dostoevsky and T. S. Eliot, awareness slowly dawned that Christianity directly addressed these things.

Fourth, a college friend, Bob Kramer, became a Christian

when we were twenty. He thought about the same kinds of questions I thought about. For the next five years we discussed, disagreed, and debated whenever we got together. I was stubborn. I could follow the plausible logic of Christian faith. But every train of thought came to the same dead end. I did not want someone to rescue me. I did not want someone to tell me what to do. I wanted to do life on my own and on my own terms. But God had other ideas about how to do my life.

How Did God Work?

He was merciful. One evening Bob spoke with unexpected candor, "I respect you as much as anyone I know . . . but what you believe . . . and how you are living . . . you are destroying yourself." I knew he was right. The Holy Spirit used his words as an armor-piercing shell. I came under comprehensive and specific conviction of my sinfulness, uncleanness, unbelief, and unacceptability before Christ. It was a my-whole-life-passing-before-my-eyes moment. I felt the weight of many sins. The two that cut me the deepest were not on the popular list of heinous transgressions. As a man with an existentialist streak, I had believed that despair, not joy, got last say. And as someone who wanted to run my own life, I had not believed the love of God in Jesus Christ, but relentlessly rejected him. I realized my wrong on both counts. When I responded (one minute later? ten minutes?), I asked, "How do I become a Christian?" Bob shared a promise from the God of hope:

> I will sprinkle clean water on you, and you shall be clean from all your uncleannesses, and from all your idols I will cleanse you. And I will give you a new heart, and a new

spirit I will put within you. And I will remove the heart of stone from your flesh and give you a heart of flesh. And I will put my Spirit within you, and cause you to walk in my statutes and be careful to obey my rules. (Ezek. 36:25–27)

Bob invited me to ask God for mercy. I beseeched God for mercy. God was merciful. Promises from eons ago proved true—God willingly saves, forgives sins, creates a new life, gives his own Spirit, promises great help to obey. He did all this. He found me and led me home. I was surprised by joy and by the love of Jesus.

When I began to read Romans a few days later, the words leapt from the page. I am one of those people that Romans 10:20 describes: the Lord showed himself to a man who was not asking for him. Though I could not follow every step of Paul's logic (a persisting phenomenon!), the gist made perfect sense:

- Sinfulness is universal and deadly—and describes me perfectly.
- Jesus Christ bore our sins and our death in his own body. He died for me.
- All lasting good depends on God's decisive initiative in showing mercy. He chose to rescue me.
- God freely pardons and justifies his enemies through faith in the Messiah. By nature, nurture, choice, and habit, I am the kind of person Romans 5 describes: weak, ungodly, sinful, his enemy. By mercy, I am the kind of person God reconciles to himself and floods with kindnesses.
- The Holy Spirit pours God's love into our hearts. He enables me to say, "Father." He goes about the business of faith, hope, love, humility, joy, and peace.

This I believe. Here I stand. Make it so. "For from him and through him and to him are all things. To him be glory forever. Amen" (Rom. 11:36).

How on Earth Did I Change?

I was changed because God intervened personally. I was changed because words of Scripture invited me into Christ. I was changed because a friend was faithful and honest. I was changed because of failure, guilt, suffering, and disillusionment. I changed because I turned from sin to Christ.

I mentioned earlier that conscious *revisiting* of justification and adoption, God's sovereignty, and identity in Christ played a relatively minor role in my Christian life. It is no doubt significant that I was dramatically converted in my midtwenties as a godless, anti-Christian adult. I had lived in such diehard opposition to Christian faith that Christ arranged this Damascus road conversion. One effect has been that God's merciful love has been a core operating assumption from the inception of my Christian life. For reasons intrinsic to my particular story, I have never doubted that I am saved from outside myself. I have simply known that God freely chooses to call us from the kingdom of death into the kingdom of life.

It has been self-evident that the Spirit is the life-giver, and we are reborn from above. I have never doubted that God forgives and justifies us by Jesus's active obedience in self-giving love, by his passive obedience in suffering death in our place, by his vindication in resurrection to indestructible life. It has been a given that the Father takes former enemies and adopts us as beloved children in the Beloved Son. It has been a working assumption that the Spirit works in us every step of the way until God completes what he has begun. God is evidently sovereign. I didn't even want to be a Christian, and he overruled. And our identity is evidently not self-generated or self-referential, because I found who I really am when I found myself in relationship with Christ. Of course, my knowledge of these things has been greatly deepened, enriched, and made articulate over the years, to my incalculable benefit. I could not have written this paragraph thirty-five years ago. My understanding and gratitude have grown. But the foundational saving realities have operated more as tacit givens than as explicit acquisitions.

Why was this? It doesn't always happen this way for people. But in my case I was grasped by the foundational truths of God's person and grace at the time of my conversion. It was a dramatic moment of decision, like what sometimes happens with a drug addict, a drunk, or some other "hardened sinner." My hardness was hardness of heart in fierce unbelief. And God was merciful to me the sinner.

Not Everyone Is Like Me

I know many Christians for whom the process of learning and relearning these foundational truths—you are justified, forgiven, and accepted by faith; your identity is in Christ; God is sovereign over all events; be faithful in the means of grace—has had, and continues to have, a crucial, life-rearranging significance. My wife, Nan, has been greatly blessed by each of these themes.

Every Christian's life story plays somewhat different music— variations in lyrics, melody, harmony, key, tempo, and instrumentation. I love that Handel's *Messiah* and "Blessed Be Your

Name" by Matt and Beth Redman are both in the repertoire of Christian faith. Redemption in Christ plays out in every story. This is how it should be. Pastoral ministry—both preaching and counseling—should relish the variety. We serve a King who makes no two snowflakes alike, and his thoughts regarding each individual are more numerous than snowflakes in a blizzard. It would be most odd if he said the exact same thing to change every one of us. It would contradict who he is and who we are.

Given the way God has chosen to work in my life, it is perhaps not surprising that I have not struggled with trying to prove myself to him by my efforts, diligence, and achievements. My characteristic flesh has never been goal- and achievement-oriented, either before or since becoming a Christian. So, for example, I have never felt obligated to take daily time to read Scripture and pray. I have never felt closer to God merely because of performing that duty or felt guilty for not doing it. I seek God daily because I need to. When I don't meet God personally, thoughtfully, and humbly, I suffer the consequences. It's analogous to forgetting to eat. I suffer because I am hungry, not because I feel guilty. "I'm hungry and I need to eat" is *different* from "I really should have eaten, and I failed again." The conscious drama, effort, and struggle of my sanctification has not turned on performance drivenness, or wondering how God could allow certain sufferings, or aspiring to find my identity in some role or achievement.

My longer learning curve has been in other areas. And that is the subject of the next chapter.

8

MY STORY (2)

The challenges in my sanctification are in areas where change has been painstaking and repetitive, rather than occurring in a dramatic moment of decision. The formation of habits of faith and love has only come through long seasons. Here are two crucibles of my longer, slower sanctification.

First, I identify with the indifference, laziness, and self-centeredness of the current "Whatever" generation, having been well nurtured and well practiced in the version of those sins endemic to the 1960s. I have had to learn to value caring for others and working to accomplish goals. I have never needed deliverance from obsessive striving after relationships and achievements. Instead, the Holy Spirit set out to teach me to value caring for people and doing things. So when I assess myself against those everyday failings that some call the "Seven Deadly Sins," the one that always stands at the top is *acedia*—the "not caring" of sloth.

Second, I identify with the discouragement and anxiety of people who suffer, who experience life's fragility, losses, failures, and threats. That's the accurate part of having an existentialist tendency. From my late teens, anxiety and *angst* hovered around the edges of my life, and I experienced several panic attacks in college. As mentioned in the previous chapter, several immediate encounters with death and dying when I was a young adult played a profound role in my eventual conversion to Christian faith. And from middle age on, I have had weakness thrust upon me. God has used acute and chronic health problems to teach me 2 Corinthians 1:2–11: we are able to help others because we are being helped. I have had to learn to trust God when I am weak. Christ's honest and sympathetic entry into our experience of weakness—yet another aspect of his suffering and death operating simultaneously with the work of atonement (Heb. 4:14–5:10)—has played a significant role in my sanctification. No surprise, Paul's story in 2 Corinthians 12 and a passel of psalms have repeatedly contributed to my growth in grace.

The Late 1970s to Mid-1980s

This next story spans a five- or six-year season of life rather than a single moment of illumination. I faced my version of the common human struggle with anxiety. During my early thirties, responsibilities multiplied rapidly. I had married Nan and finished seminary and was in the first years of vocational ministry. Counseling was hard. Teaching was hard. Writing was hard. I was working on a PhD at the University of Pennsylvania. Graduate study was hard. I was serving as an active elder in a church with great pastoral needs. Being an elder was hard. We were welcoming the arrival of our children and living communally with another young family with whom we shared home ownership. I needn't say more about what life is like! This cumulation of outward pressures correlated to inward stressing.

How Did God Work?

God spoke into and acted upon my harried, anxious experience. He addressed me pointedly, repeatedly, and patiently over days, months, and years. A suite of complementary truths slowly took root, blossomed, and bore fruit.

"Cast all your anxiety on him because he cares for you" (1 Pet. 5:7 NIV). Stressed people need simple. "You matter to him" is simple. But it took time for me to take that to heart. "Off-load what concerns you" is simple. But it took time to learn how to do that. I vividly remember a moment when my pastor recognized my fretfulness during a season when I was facing many pressures. He said, "Grace means courage." And he prayed for me. He cast my cares upon the One who cares, and I've never forgotten his words.

"When my anxious thoughts multiply within me, / Your consolations delight my soul" (Ps. 94:19 NASB). That first clause nails what stress, preoccupation, and anxiety feel like. The second clause invites me to look out in a different direction. The rest of Psalm 94 emphatically promises consolations. If the Lord will make right the very worst wrongs, then how much more my small troubles and pressures. This was not cognitive restructuring by changing my self-talk. Instead, it meant seeking and finding the person who actively looks out for my well-being.

"The Lord is at hand; do not be anxious about anything, but in everything by prayer and supplication with thanksgiving let your requests be made known to God" (Phil. 4:5–6). It is a huge help to remember that the One who cares and makes a difference is near. Name your troubles. Ask for help. Voice your thanks. Prayer means asking. Supplication means really asking—and meaning what you say. It is a huge help to get specific. It is a huge help to talk out loud. I learned to take all this to heart thirty years ago. I am helped right now by taking it to heart today.

"Do not be anxious about tomorrow, for tomorrow will be anxious for itself. Sufficient for the day is its own trouble" (Matt. 6:34). Your Father knows and will give what you need, so put first things first. Focus on today's concerns and calling. During a particularly harried season, a friend helped me to re-phrase it: "Sufficient for this five minutes are the troubles and concerns of this five minutes!" God himself met me through many complementary insights, messages, and messengers.

That season of life was the most conscious, intentional sea-son of change I've known. I learned to identify specific situational triggers for my anxiety. I learned how anxiety presumes a great distance between God and my present concerns. I learned how anxiety puts distance between me and others—it is the opposite of loving people. I learned to identify deviant motives: self-trust, overconcern for the opinions of others, desire to control outcomes, love of ease—all these erase God and make this *my* universe, not his. I learned to know, need, and trust God's defining attitudes and consistent ways of loving his children. I learned a fruitful wisdom that thoughtfully ponders both Scripture and life—a wisdom that prays honestly, relies on friends, and takes small constructive actions.

These were also years when I was learning to counsel others. There is a reason that "Don't be afraid" (in all its variants) is the most common command in all of Scripture. God's children struggle to live well in an unwell, unstable world. In part, this is because we ourselves drift into the unwellness and instability of living anxiously. He meets you, stabilizes you, walks with you, and makes it well with your soul. You become able to help others with the help you are receiving for yourself.

How Did I Change?

I was changed because God intervened personally, repeatedly, patiently. I was changed because Scripture's words of care and consolation invited me to my Father. I was changed because many friends were faithful and wise in how they spoke into my life. I was changed because of struggling with the pressures of life and uneasy feelings. I changed because I turned away from living as though I walked alone in a difficult universe, and I turned to the Lord who is near.

9

THE STORY OF CHARLES

In the course of teaching and counseling, I have asked many people to talk or write about *how* God drew them to seek and know him, *how* he changed them. I've asked them to describe, as far as possible, the significant and decisive factors. "As you look back on your growth as a Christian, who and what most influenced you?" Invariably, people tell stories.

The stories exhibit the features we have been exploring. Most stories begin by telling about a challenging, troubling, disorienting situation. The person faces a personal struggle with sins, disturbing emotions, confusion. And something from and about God proves to be illuminating and reorienting: who he is, his purposes, his promises, his commands. Usually other people appear somewhere in the story. Another person's trustworthy love or striking character embodies faith, gives a glimpse of Christ, and helps to mediate truth. All these elements come together and something clicks. The world looks different. The person gains a fresh understanding of God, self, and situation. A change of heart takes place, a turning to God in awakened faith, new actions of wisdom and obedience. And either explicitly or implicitly, people communicate an awareness that God himself had a hand in how all this came together. People do not tell I-did-it stories but he-did-something stories.

We are privileged to hear excerpts from those unwritten books that bear witness to what Jesus does. This chapter and the next will present and discuss two stories of change. These stories are typical in that they contain features that recur in every redemption story. Yet they are idiosyncratic in that they demonstrate the individuality and local color of any good story.[1]

Overcoming Betrayal

Charles is a single man in his early thirties, a well-taught layman, active in his Asian-American church, a computer programmer by profession. He writes:

> Recently I have returned often to Ps. 119:86: "All your commandments are faithful; they persecute me with a lie; help me!" Immediately, it says to me that there is such a thing as *completely* and *always* trustworthy. Especially in recently experiencing being sinned against by broken trust, gossip, and betrayal . . . I cling to the truth that God is always trustworthy and what he says to me is trustworthy. He helps me to trust again. When I say, "Help me!" I *know* I'm talking with my Father, even in the midst of facing broken trust from people who hurt me, who don't even think there's a problem, who don't even want to try to resolve it. It's like I'm dealing with a cover-up. Everybody seems to be avoid-

ing what happened. When I try to bring it up, *I'm* viewed as the problem because I want to name and resolve what happened, not just pretend.

It's so hard to forgive in this situation. It's easy to grumble inside, to get caught up in my dark, fiery emotions, to replay the video of what happened, to get bitter and paranoid around my group of friends. Sometimes I just pack it in, and surf the web checking out sports cars and ecotourist adventures. I have a new sympathy for why someone might just chuck the church and become a drunk. But Jesus calls me to forgive from the heart. Mark 11:25 is open and shut: one of God's faithful commands. I know that's where I need to go, if I'm to come out of this as a constructive person, not destructive or self-destructive. And I'm getting there. God is faithful. *God . . . is . . . faithful.* Jesus truly forgives me when I struggle. As I confess my bitterness and grumbling, he truly helps me. I need him to clear my head in order to sort out what I need to do next, and so I can do it in the right way and not just tangle things up more.

Thinking about Charles's Story

Hearing such a story is like catching the flash of a goldfinch on the wing. We are privileged to enter into a man's life as it is happening. What are we seeing and hearing?

The passage Charles cites explicitly names a common life situation: verbal mistreatment by another person. Notice, there's not necessarily a perfect one-to-one fit between this Scripture and Charles's life, but it's close enough to be relevant.[2] A subsequent conversation with Charles revealed what had happened. A long-standing friend and trusted confidant had betrayed his trust. The friend had gossiped a sensitive confidence, degrading Charles in the eyes of their circle of fellowship. In the psalm, the persecutory liars are identified as enemies of both God and the psalmist, people never to be trusted, who threaten literal death and destruction. In Charles's situation, the sense of threat— "death and destruction"—was metaphorical, a devastating estrangement in social relations.

The pain and perplexity were aggravated because there had been real trust, and this trust was betrayed. The offense came not from an enemy but from a brother in Christ who treated him in an enemy-like manner, and then tried to smooth it over by acting like nothing happened. The particular "lie" was actually a factual statement, but a true statement used maliciously becomes falsehood. The situational reference contained in Psalm 119:86 is appropriate and relevant, but Charles has intuitively done something quite intricate in connecting it to what happened to him.

The internal struggle provoked by being sinned against is only implicit in the actual words of Psalm 119:86. But a sense of personal distress, affliction, temptation to reactive sin, and need for help are obvious, both from universal human experience as implied in the cry for help, and as illustrated throughout Psalm 119 and the rest of Scripture. Charles legitimately reads his unhappiness and his problematic reactions back into the passage: "They persecute me with a lie [*and I feel threatened, overwhelmed, hurt, frustrated in all my efforts, unhappy, and I am tempted to be angry, fearful, escapist and mistrusting*]." We witness his version of the universal struggle with double evil: evils come upon us and evils come from within us. Mistreatment occasions many temptations, and Charles's story candidly expresses his experience of trial and temptation. We witness— and feel—his need for help. His Scripture passage of choice comfortably contains many variations on the human theme, including his own.

And then there is the revelation of God. The Lord never tells all in any one moment of self-revelation. Various aspects of God's person, purposes, character, will, promises, and actions come onto the table in various portions of Scripture: always timely to the complexities of a particular situation, always pointedly appropriate to the perplexities of existential choice for a particular person or people.

Here in Psalm 119:86, we hear one truth and overhear another: God's directive words are true and faithful, and he is a helper on whom the needy may call. In Charles's story—again, a typical application of Scripture, generating an encounter with God and ethical transformation—we hear not only the overt revelation in this one verse but also numerous echoes, conflations, and allusions arising from the biblical backstory. This wider context shapes Charles's reception of Psalm 119:86. For example, the verse per se does not mention the Father, or the work of Jesus, or the forgiveness of our sins, or the command of Mark 11:25, or the goal of coming out into daylight as a constructive human being. But the verse easily bears such fine gifts to a man in his need.

Notice also how God's revelation always attaches promises to his commands and attaches commands to his promises. He gives us grace upon grace; he calls us to know him and become like him. In Charles's story, the truths that echo in the background always tie trustworthy reasons to trustworthy commands:

- Forgive (standard) as you have been forgiven in Christ (God's person, work, promise).
- Take refuge (standard) in your Rock and Shepherd, who is a safe place for the afflicted (a train of evocative reasons).
- Be an imitator (standard) of God as a beloved child (a cornucopia of promises), and walk in love (standard) as Christ loved us and gave himself up for us, an offering and a sacrifice to God as a fragrant aroma (the propitiatory burnt offering of the Lamb, whose fragrance soothes and pleases God).

In technical language, the indicative (what is true about and from God) always frames and drives the imperative (how we are to respond). Faith works through love. Trust begets obedience.

Charles's troubles and struggles come together with a revelation of who God is, and Charles turns from the world of sin and death to the God of grace and life. Charles turns—and is still turning. A change occurs in Charles—and recurs. It is not one and done. Charles continues to engage his ongoing situation in the light of and by the power of the normative Redeemer Lord. We hear faith working all through his story: "I have returned often . . . Immediately, it says to me . . . I cling . . . He helps me to trust again. When I say, "Help me!" I *know* I'm talking with my Father . . . I know that's where I need to go . . . *God . . . is . . . faithful . . .* When I confess . . . he truly helps me." Notice the active verbs, his italics, and the immediacy of relationship.

This example contains all vertical transformation so far, but Charles is in motion toward horizontal transformation as well. He is working out the "attitudinal" forgiveness (Matt. 6:12–15; Mark 11:25) that is the precondition for constructively approaching another person to work toward "transacted" forgiveness (Matt. 18:15–17; Luke 17:3–4).

Note several further implications. First, Charles is changing, but the story isn't over. The renewal of our lives is not our arriving at an ideal of ethical perfection, moral self-improvement, or blissful equanimity. There are people Charles must talk with. Much good has been happening, but the process is still ongoing, and the outcome remains indeterminate. Charles is moving to the next phase of struggle. We rejoice at what we witness so far. But we sit on the edge of our chairs, waiting with eager longing to see if peacemakers will sow peace, bringing to further realization the ethical glory of the sons of God. What happens next is fraught with uncertainty. How will the former friend respond? How will the wider circle of friends respond? Will church leaders step in helpfully if the situation continues unresolved? Will Charles go forward in the light? Or will he regress into bitterness, self-pity, and fantasizing over Corvettes? His life is a holy experiment. In the long run, the grace and goodness of God will finally triumph. But the resolution of this situation is still uncertain.

Second, in subsequent conversations Charles mentioned something that does not appear in his initial story. He feels alone in his church, but he is not alone. He is being significantly helped by several men who now live outside the area. With some frequency Charles connects with a former pastor and with a friend from his college InterVarsity group. They have been helping him to stay centered on God's purposes. He trusts them. And they have shown themselves trustworthy by the care, confidentiality, candor, and prayerfulness with which they are responding to him in his struggles.

Third, the cure of our souls usually involves a different sort of ethical judgment than the analyses and judgments pertaining to depersonalized ethical cases and moral dilemmas. To move forward, Charles needs more than coming to a thoughtful Christian *position* about what he ought to do. Most ethical discourse is topical—for example, abortion, just war, homosexuality, the definition of marriage, grounds for divorce, medical decision making. It only occasionally reaches down into the grit of personal struggles and daily pastoral care. Even an analysis of matters immediately pertinent to Charles's situation does not plumb the intricacies of personal and pastoral need. How should a Christian respond to violation of trust by a brother? When and how is it right for a church to intervene in a conflict in order to help reconcile, adjudicate, advocate, and discipline? Those topical ethical judgments frame the cure of souls, but they don't carry the process along. Martin Luther cogently captures how the Christian life is a dynamic process, not a static attainment:

> This life, therefore, is not righteousness but growth in righteousness, not health but healing, not being but becoming, not rest but exercise. We are not yet what we shall be, but we are growing toward it. The process is not yet finished but it is going on. This is not the end but it is the road. All does not yet gleam in glory but all is being purified.[3]

The Christian *position* defines right and wrong, sets boundary conditions and goals, and can be relatively tidy. But the Christian *process* struggles forward amid many variables, contingencies, and uncertainties.

Fourth, we have looked closely at how the various factors in Charles's life actually come together. It shows by contrast how so much typical advice fails to connect the dots for people. When specifics of the real-life story are left off the table, our counsel to Charles is reduced to a doctrinal, moralistic, pietistic, or therapeutic exhortation:

- Give your troubles to Jesus.
- Get into counseling.
- Remember God's sovereignty.
- Take medication.
- Affirm that you're a child of the King.
- Get involved in a small group.
- Explore how your family of origin affected you.
- Attend to the means of grace.
- Have a mountaintop experience.
- Get into an accountability relationship.
- Change churches and get a new set of friends.
- Cast out the demon of bitterness.
- Count your blessings.
- Repent of bitterness and love your enemy.
- Go to the person, and if he won't listen, take one or two others with you.
- Take this key verse, Psalm 119:86, and pray the Ezer Prayer ("Help me") every day, claiming your victory. This verse opens God's storehouse of blessing. (I'll admit I made up this one.)

Some of this counsel would contribute well when functioning as part of a larger, more personal whole. Other bits of counsel are nonsense, inappropriate, mystifying, or misleading. And none of these bits captures the reality of that linkage between external troubles, internal struggles, wise friends, and the actively hands-on, self-revealing Shepherd of our souls. None of these captures what actually is helping Charles. They lack feel for the process of living as a Christian, for what it is like to be a human being under the care of Christ. The reorientation of a human being never comes via pat answers or quick fixes. Charles illustrates something better, something richer, more human, more humane, and truer to Scripture and life.

10

THE STORY OF CHARLOTTE

Our final story is more intricate biblically, more complex situationally, and richer experientially. Charlotte is a female seminary student in her midtwenties and single, with intuitive counseling skills. Let me set the stage by some comparison with the previous case study.

You will see that the similarities are basic: both stories reveal how a reorientation and transformation take place. But the time line for Charles's story was relatively short: an experience in the immediate past, still churning in the present, and calling for further action in the immediate future. Charlotte's story will come to a point in the present, but it reflects retrospectively on a long history.

Charles faced immediate situational stressors and struggled against immediate sinful responses. But Charlotte wrestles with larger forces: long-standing patterns of how she comes at life; the fundamental discomfort of the human condition; contradictions operative in herself, in her experience of the church, and in relation to non-Christians.

The change process in Charles was linear, a succession of specific sins against him, specific sinful responses, a specific promise and command of God, the encouragement of wise friends, transactions of repentance and faith, and an anticipation of very specific behavioral fruit. The changes you will see in Charlotte are more atmospheric, and she bears rich and complex fruit. We hear a particularly deep intimacy in her relationship to God. She makes one striking behavioral change. There are certain transformations that might be termed internal fruit: a subtle reorientation in how she understands herself, her situation, her God; a refinement in how her conscience functions; a linguistic richness that captures the poetry of experience, making her relationship with God come to life for us.

No Longer Insecure

Here are Charlotte's words:

> I've returned a lot to Isaiah 51:12–13b and 15–16.
>
>> I, I am he who comforts you;
>>> who are you that you are afraid of man who dies,
>>> of the son of man who is made like grass,
>> and have forgotten the LORD, your Maker,
>>> who stretched out the heavens
>>> and laid the foundations of the earth,
>> and you fear continually all the day . . . ?
>> I am the LORD your God,
>>> who stirs up the sea so that its waves roar—
>>> the LORD of hosts is his name.

> And I have put my words in your mouth
>> and covered you in the shadow of my hand,
> establishing the heavens
>> and laying the foundations of the earth,
>> and saying to Zion, "You are my people."

This reminds me that this world is not a "comfortable" one, and assures me that Christ is the only true comfort (despite those things I try to fill in to comfort me instead). It lends confidence to not be afraid of what those around me are thinking about me—freedom to live transparently. The awareness that I am always forgetting about God stings my cheeks. I'm an amnesiac to his sovereignty and grace in the world and in my life.

These verses so insanely juxtapose and bind together the hugeness of Creator God and the close intimacy of Christ. He is incomprehensibly vast and powerful. He stretched out the heavens and laid the foundations of the earth; he stirs the roaring waves; he is LORD of hosts; and, again—in case I missed it the first time—he establishes the heavens and lays the foundations of the earth. In the exact same breath, he is wonderfully intimate. "I, I am he who comforts." I can't get over that double-I. He made me; he puts his very words in my mouth; his hand covers me; he says, "You are my people."

Somehow life makes the MOST sense in the middle of this tension and seeming paradox of God's identity. I feel it on the deepest level of my relationship with God. I am also comforted when I see how this parallels other tensions, confusions and contradictions both around me and within me. God is not tidy, all black and white with straight-lines, fitting into a box—and neither am I—and knowing that is an affirmation and a comfort!

I was always intimidated by people and their possible opinions of me—intimidated by everybody except my Mom. But last week in a missions class, I had to hold my tongue because I was dominating the conversation for most of the 3 hour discussion. It's all coming out, after being hemmed in by fear for all those years of awkward insecurity!

Thinking about Charlotte's Story

My discussion of Charlotte's story will be brief, as many of the points made about Charles are also applicable here. But for starters, simply savor this story as a story. Read it again and let it sink in. There is more to it than my analysis can point out or capture.

Notice the variety of situational troubles on the table. In the foreground: the potential disapproval of others in every social situation. In the wider context: that this is an essentially uncomfortable world; some unspecified sense of "tensions, confusions and contradictions . . . around me." From subsequent conversation, I learned that Charlotte is alluding to brushing up against self-righteous pettiness in an ecclesiastical conflict, and to her encounter with theological dogmatism in hard-edged people who seemed to not really understand God, or themselves, or others, or life. She is also alluding to the sense of contradiction she experiences when instances of hypocrisy and inhumanity in Christian people are juxtaposed with instances of honesty, care, and humanity in non-Christians.

Notice the subtlety of Charlotte's inner, personal struggles. In the foreground: Charlotte's atmospheric fear of man, shyness, social anxiety, and withdrawal. In the background: discouragement and confusion in the face of both what is around her and her inner struggles. She feels out of step with some of the comfortable verities of her evangelical subculture. She also alludes to the false comforts to which she turns as easy substitutes for Christ: self-medicating through food, exercise, friends, and novels.

Notice the revelation of our Redeemer—this most magnificent, most comforting God of Isaiah 51. He tells her not to be afraid (the one command), which Charlotte intuitively extends to include its positive meanings: enter in, get involved, care, speak up. Isaiah 51 gives her a cascade of good reasons: the reproofs of 51:12 that sting her cheeks; the many wonders and intimacies that comfort her "on the deepest level." Charlotte is a living demonstration of how faith and works cooperate in response to God's vivid self-revelation.

As in the passage that so impacted Charles, the Scripture that Charlotte mentions—ported forward from a very different redemptive-historical context and personalized—seems uniquely appropriate. It is "close enough" for relevance. She reads and appropriates this passage by peopling it with her own experience and by enriching it with echoes and allusions from the person and work of Christ.

Finally, notice the dynamic of change. God, the situation, Charlotte's struggles, and her faith all come together in a context that had always been anxiety-producing and intimidating for her. A new and living reality emerges. A transformative engagement occurs between strong Savior and needy child: stinging cheeks at realizing her amnesia, the experience of deep comfort. The behavioral consequences are striking: new freedom to live and speak transparently, a conscience newly sensitized to the dangers of talking too much. Her newfound voice is particularly significant. Action registers that change is real.

Charlotte's story also illustrates several other features of the cure of souls. First, change is a lifelong process in which we witness thematic continuities. In the classroom incident, God was rescripting patterns that go back to childhood. Sin is usually not newly hatched; righteousness doesn't fall like random fire from heaven. As you get to know a person, you learn to see patterns and themes in the interplay of existential and situational factors, just as students of Scripture learn to see patterns and themes in the Bible. It helps a person to know that the Vinedresser is pruning purposefully. It greatly helps all of us to know that God typically works on *something* specific, not everything at once.

Second, I learned something else about Charlotte when I followed up on that throwaway line about her mother. Her father had abandoned the family when Charlotte was very young, but her mother had been a lifelong rock of refuge. They had a loving, honest relationship.

> We can talk about anything. I *know* my mother is on my side. And I also know that she'll encourage me, and that when she challenges me, it's something I need to hear and it comes from love. A lot of what I've been learning in this season of growth fits with how she lives her life, and with

things she has said to me and prayed for me. But I had to learn it and own it for myself as an adult.

Her mother is not an immediate catalyst in how Charlotte is growing. But Mom's background influence is significant and unquantifiable.

Third, how is it that Charlotte and I view her "speaking up" as a fruit of the Spirit? That item is not on any list of fruit (though I think it's implicitly among the "such things" of Gal. 5:23). We know it is good fruit because we understand her situational troubles and personal struggles in the light of revelation. Fear of man coached Charlotte to stay in the background, to play it safe. In social groups, she was virtually a nonparticipant, unable to bring her thoughts to the point of joining in audibly. She was self-preoccupied, not loving. She was fearful, not free. As the fruit of repentance and faith, the Spirit freed her to participate. He loosens her tongue, because that is what love and obedience now look like in Charlotte's life.

Fourth, Charlotte's ironic, humorous sensibility of the need to hold her tongue captures other features of the Christian life. It's evidence that her conscience is alive, sensitive, malleable. Such bursts of intuitive wisdom are unscriptable and electrifying—and are one aspect of ethical transformation into wisdom.

Fifth, needing to hold her tongue also illustrates how the cure of any living soul calls for continual course correction. She finds her voice and immediately realizes that there are sins of the tongue and that there are times when love quiets down and listens. It's a new lesson.

Sixth, in this ironic combination of learning to speak up

and needprocing to quiet down, Charlotte is tasting the logic of Luther's curious exhortation, "Sin boldly!" Step out, live life, and yet always be open to correction. Don't let scrupulosity paralyze action. God's mercies are reliably "new every morning" (Lam. 3:22–23). As with a good mother or father, the Lord's compassion and hands-on parenting continue through the ups and downs. The Christian life typically lurches forward rather than marching uniformly in a straight line. The patient grace of Christ means a person can live life without paralyzing perfectionism and obsessive self-examination. We can cheerfully, humbly expect frequent life lessons. Charlotte has always held back in social settings. Now that she's beginning to speak up, she'll probably say things she regrets, or may find herself talking too much. It's safer to hang in the background and nod agreeably (cf. Prov. 17:28 on the fool who keeps silent!). It's risky to mix it up. She'll make mistakes, even sinning verbally (James 3:2). Other people won't always agree with her if Charlotte doesn't seem to always agree with them. She'll have to learn to face and solve conflicts rather than always avoiding conflict. She'll have to ask forgiveness more often. She might sin "more," but she'll actually be sinning less and growing up as a daughter of the King. She will always need course corrections.

"God meets you where you are." That's a truism. But when you stop and ponder *how* that happens and *why* it happens, it is nothing less than light breaking into darkness. A sin-sick, life-bruised soul revives and begins to live. God said, "Let light shine out of darkness" at the creation of the universe (2 Cor. 4:6). In the re-creation, this same God shines into our hearts, awakening us to behold the glory of God in the face of Jesus Christ. The

Christian life is organically alive. We turn, we trust, we obey, we grow—interacting with what's happening around us, as the God of truth breaks in. He has gathered us to himself in a lifelong holy experiment in redemption. Charles and Charlotte teach us something of that dynamic.

11

THE JOURNEY

Because learning how to live is the most complex skill imaginable, the struggle will not cease until you and I have faced our last enemy and we see the face of God. Meanwhile, we live as travelers. We walk. When we see God, faith will become sight and love will no longer be difficult. All relationships will be uncomplicated. We will no longer need to learn endurance, forbearance, patience, perseverance, forgiveness, repentance, peacemaking, and all the other things that are so important on our journey home.

In these chapters, we have been considering the meaning of sanctification, which is Christ's working purpose on our journey. You have probably noticed that we have continually returned to considering our relationships, first with God and then with others. It seems fitting to conclude with a reprise to faith and a reprise to love.

Faith

Lines from John Newton's "Amazing Grace" deftly capture the difficulties of our journey, the attractiveness of our destination, and the characteristics of the One who is leading us to his own home:

> Through many dangers, toils, and snares
>> I have already come;
> 'Tis grace hath brought me safe thus far,
>> and grace will lead me home.

How did Newton come to understand that? His work distills comforts and encouragements that Psalm 23 instills in our hearts:

> The Lord is my shepherd; I shall not want.
>> He makes me lie down in green pastures.
> He leads me beside still waters.
>> He restores my soul.
> He leads me in paths of righteousness
>> for his name's sake.

> Even though I walk through the valley of the
>> shadow of death,
>> I will fear no evil,
> for you are with me;
>> your rod and your staff,
>> they comfort me.

> You prepare a table before me
>> in the presence of my enemies;

you anoint my head with oil;
   my cup overflows.
Surely goodness and mercy shall follow me
   all the days of my life,
and I shall dwell in the house of the LORD forever.

John Newton knew this was true and put it in his own words.

If your life is in fact a journey, then Psalm 23 maps the route and reminds you about the company you keep. Our companion is alert, amiable, generous, and strong. He willingly walks with us. He is looking out for us. We face troubles of many kinds. But he will never leave us or forsake us. We know from other Scripture that this Shepherd even laid down his life for his beloved sheep. And we know that we are his sheep because we recognize his voice speaking to us. We know he is taking us to his home.

That is one kind of journey. But life can go other ways. Psalm 1 keys the entire book of Psalms by inviting each of us to ask, "How will my life turn out? What will happen to me?" Not all the answers are happy. Some ways of living come to be nothing but chaff and can be blown away into nothingness by a puff of wind. Macbeth had an inkling:

   . . . full of sound and fury,
   signifying nothing.[1]

That's what remains of life when we remove the Lord's presence. Without a Good Shepherd, we script our lives to the opposite of Psalm 23, to an antipsalm of foolish hopes. Life is still a journey, and we still head toward a destination; the difficulties and threats along the way are identical. But everything else is different. Antipsalms build a life journey on the premise that the Lord is not present and active. Here are the premises that orient a popular contemporary version of the antipsalm. It starts out with a heady, self-confident affirmation of faith:

- I can take care of myself.
- I am basically a good person.
- I can pursue and achieve my goals.
- I am confident in myself and my abilities.
- I say what I think and do what I want.

But in the long run, like all the antipsalms, this faith betrays its believers. When the Lord is not your Shepherd, the outcome and destination are predictable:

- I am alone. No one looks out for me or looks after me.
- I am empty, needy, restless, and unsafe.
- When I walk through the valley of the shadow of death, I have no protector.
- I fear the bad things that can happen to me.
- Other people let you down or hurt you.
- In the end you lose every good thing you ever had.
- Death is my shepherd.[2]

The antipsalm comes to a dead end in the valley of the shadow of death.

So which faith will it be? Every person experiences hardships on the journey. All of us live under the shadow of death. All of us face many evils. Live any one of the antipsalms, and in the end all is loss. But live Psalm 23, and you will find that you awaken one day and say with joy, "I'm home!"

Love

It's easy to view sanctification as a moral self-improvement project. It's easy to think that God's goal is just to make me a better individual than I am now. I hope this short book has disabused you of that notion. Yes, of course, we're our own worst enemies—prone to a turbulent cocktail of anxieties, complaining, deceptiveness, selfishness, compulsions, irritability, confusion, indifference, immorality, self-righteousness, low self-esteem, judgmentalism, money loving, laziness, drivenness, "and things like these" (to quote Gal. 5:21). But the Lord's desired outcome is not simply a better me who has found peace and gotten his act together.

The goal of sanctification is not a better, happier, more confident individual—not exactly. Listen to how Scripture puts it:

"The Father of mercies and God of all comfort . . . comforts us in all our affliction, so that we may be able to comfort those who are in any affliction" (2 Cor. 1:4). When you find hope and encouragement in your troubles, the comfort doesn't land with you just feeling better. You now have riches to bring to others in whatever troubles they experience. Their welfare and yours have joined hands. The well-being of others increasingly matters as you become a participating member of Christ's body, brothers and sisters in our Father's family. Sanctification is making you into a person who is connected, wedded, and joined to Jesus Christ and all the other people whose center of gravity is shifting outside themselves.

"He can deal gently with the ignorant and wayward, since he himself is beset with weakness. Because of this he is obligated

to offer sacrifice for his own sins just as he does for those of the people" (Heb. 5:2–3). Knowing how gently God deals with you in your confusion, short-sightedness, and wanderings, you deal gently with others in their sins and weaknesses. It is wonderful to experience that God is gracious, compassionate, slow to anger, abounding in steadfast love and faithfulness, forgiving your iniquity, transgression, and sin. And as you learn that he is this way with you in your ignorance and waywardness, you develop the same heart for others in their failings. You aren't simply a "happier person." This world is too full of woes and woebegone people. You take the pains and confusion of others to heart. You are becoming a person sobered by the human condition and willing to help.

"Be kind to one another, tenderhearted, forgiving one another, as God in Christ forgave you. Therefore be imitators of God, as beloved children. And walk in love, as Christ loved us and gave himself up for us, a fragrant offering and sacrifice to God" (Eph. 4:32–5:2). Forgiven people don't simply rest in peace because their restless sins, corrosive guilt, and dark shame are now covered. You now have goodness and mercy to bring to others. Knowing that you are a beloved child does not leave you complacent and self-satisfied. You are beloved so that you are able to love, to give your life away for others. You don't become a "self-confident individual." Your life might be stressful. You serve the King and Savior who died at age thirty-three—and his service is not always convenient. It puts you out of your comfort zone. It strips away all the illusions that we can control people and events. You are becoming a person whose confidence rests

outside yourself in God, a person whose life purpose is Christ's purpose of redeeming love.

You are giving away what is being given to you. Trust, thankfulness, and worship to the God who gives. Care, wisdom, and mercies to people in need. Many psalms open on a personal note, pleading with God for one's own sins and sorrows. They close by pleading for others. Mercy received becomes mercy to give. The words "image of Christ" can tumble from our lips without us understanding how Jesus is the man for God and for others. He identifies himself with the needs, sins, sorrows, and weaknesses of others. His life purpose is to bring redemption into the dark, hard places where redemption is needed. Being found by him, we know how others need finding.

B. B. Warfield put these things so well:

Christ was led by His love for others into the world, to forget Himself in the needs of others, to sacrifice self once for all upon the altar of sympathy. Self-sacrifice brought Christ into the world. And self-sacrifice will lead us, His followers, not away from but into the midst of men.

Wherever men suffer, there will we be to comfort. Wherever men strive, there will we be to help. Wherever men fail, there will we be to uplift. Wherever men succeed, there will we be to rejoice. Self-sacrifice means not indifference to our times and our fellows: it means absorption in them. It means forgetfulness of self in others. It means entering into every man's hopes and fears, longings and despairs: it means manysidedness of spirit, multiform activity, multiplicity of sympathies. It means richness of development.

It means not that we should live one life, but a thousand lives—binding ourselves to a thousand souls by the filaments of so loving a sympathy that their lives become ours. It means that all the experiences of men shall smite our souls and shall beat and batter these stubborn hearts of ours into fitness for their heavenly home. It is, after all, then, the path to the highest possible development, by which alone we can be made truly men.[3]

May a loving sympathy beat and batter these stubborn hearts of ours into fitness for our heavenly home. Faith and love are the fruit of the Spirit's sanctifying grace. You are no longer an isolated individual, divided off from others, an island of self-reliance. You are becoming a person, bound together for life with your brothers and sisters.

Perhaps the most dramatic evidence of headway in sanctification is that you no longer think so much about yourself. You are starting to do better when you are not preoccupied with "How well am I doing?" You are finding yourself when you lose yourself and worry less about who you are. A sinner forgiven, a sufferer sheltered, a saint in process—your welfare is inextricable from our welfare together.

We are one in Christ. We are heading home. We will see his face. And all will be made well.

NOTES

Introduction

1. In the Bible itself, the word *sanctify* is most often used in the past tense. It describes something that has already happened. It is one way of describing how God decisively acts to make you his own. You *were washed*, you *were sanctified*, you *were justified* in the name of the Lord Jesus Christ and by the Spirit of our God. You *are* chosen, holy, and beloved. You *have been made alive* together with Christ. God in Christ *forgave* you. You *have received* the Spirit of adoption as sons, by whom we cry, "Abba! Father!" You *are* a chosen race, a royal priesthood, a holy nation, a people for his own possession. He *called* you out of darkness into his marvelous light. You *are sanctified* in Christ Jesus and *called* saints, together with all those who in every place call upon the name of our Lord Jesus Christ. In all these ways, the Bible affirms that you already belong to God. See Rom. 8:15; 1 Cor. 1:2; 6:11; Eph. 2:5; 4:32; Col. 3:12; 1 Pet. 2:9.

2. Parts of this book appeared in earlier form in David Powlison, "How Does Sanctification Work?," parts 1–3, *Journal of Biblical Counseling* 27, no. 1 (2013): 49–66; *JBC* 27, no. 2 (2013): 35–50; *JBC* 31, no. 1 (2017): 9–32; Powlison, "Frame's Ethics: Working the Implications for Pastoral Care," in *Speaking the Truth in Love: The Theology of John M. Frame*, ed. John J. Hughes (Phillipsburg, NJ: P&R, 2009), 759–77; and Powlison, "How Does Scripture Change You?," *JBC* 26, no. 2 (2012): 26–32.

Chapter 1. God Meets Us with His Promises

1. I have been greatly enriched by reading thoughtful reflections from several thousand students who have detailed the truths, the people, and the circumstances that most influenced their growth in grace. Two of their stories will appear in later chapters of this book.

Chapter 2. Is There One Key to Sanctification?
1. This popular teaching is my immediate case study, but my larger intention is to address any and all forms of reductionism.
2. Of course, Christians significantly differ over how the details work! Faithful people differ about how to rightly and helpfully express the categories, priorities, ordering, emphases, wording, and definitions. I have my views, but for the purposes of this book, it is enough to assert the areas of broad agreement.

Chapter 3. Truth Unbalanced and Rebalanced
1. I am indebted to my friend James Petty for this basic insight.

Chapter 4. God Meets Us with His Commands
1. Patrick O'Brian, *The Surgeon's Mate* (New York: W. W. Norton, 1981), 282.

Chapter 5. We Are Sanctified by Remembering Our Justification
1. This doesn't invalidate the application made in the previous paragraphs. As pastoral work so often does, that application was by implication and extension, rather than the exact application made by the text.

Chapter 6. What Changes You?
1. These are attributed to Oliver Wendell Holmes Sr. and to Addison Leitch, respectively. But like many bits of proverbial wisdom, the attributions are hard to verify.
2. The sacraments similarly express the dynamic interplay between God himself and the words and elements (bread, wine, and water) that are bearers of his promise, presence, and strength. We participate by receiving and responding.
3. It is also true that non-Christians can profoundly affect us for good because of God's common grace. I have learned many things from non-Christians about hospitality, hard work, beauty, patience, language, courage, and scholarly integrity.
4. It is a less developed theme in Scripture, but blessings and happy circumstances can also change us for the good—when we have learned to see God's hand in them and are grateful.

Chapter 9. The Story of Charles
1. Each is based primarily on one person's written story, slightly modified in three ways. First, identifying details have been altered. Second, I have supplemented the discussion with further knowledge gained in pastoral conversations. Third, I have woven in some particulars from other people whose experience was analogous, thus creating a composite case.

2. "Close enough" relevance is "analogical" relevance. This involves hermeneutical and ethical intricacies that are far easier to illustrate than to state. See chap. 7 in John M. Frame, *The Doctrine of the Knowledge of God* (Phillipsburg, NJ: P&R, 1987), 215–41, for a careful discussion.
3. Martin Luther, "Defense and Explanation of All the Articles, 1521," in *Career of the Reformer II*, vol. 32 of *Luther's Works*, American Edition, ed. Jaroslav Pelikan and Helmut T. Lehmann (Philadelphia: Augsburg Fortress, 1958), 24.

Chapter 11. The Journey

1. William Shakespeare, *The Tragedy of Macbeth*, act 5, scene 5.
2. I borrowed this last line from Ps. 49:14, paraphrasing it to fit the first-person experience of the antipsalm.
3. Benjamin B. Warfield, "Imitating the Incarnation" (sermon), in *The Person and Work of Christ*, ed. Samuel Craig (Philadelphia: Presbyterian and Reformed, 1950), 574–75.

GENERAL INDEX

abstraction, theological categories as, 25, 29
accountability relationships, 24
acedia, 79
"Amazing Grace" (hymn), 106
analogical relevance, 115n2 (chap. 9)
angst, 80
antipsalms, 107–8
anxiety, 57, 80–82
apple of God's eye, 19, 31
application, to particular persons and situations, 24
attitudinal forgiveness, 91

balancing. *See also* unbalancing
art of, 40–42
organic unity of, 50
betrayal, 86–90
biblical theology, 40

change, 61–69, 96, 100
Christian life
as biographical and theological, 15–16
as dynamic process, 92–93, 102–3
enriched in the mundane, 20
generalizations of, 50–51

as struggle, 54
Christus Victor, 36
comfort, 96–98, 99
in the cross, 35–36
commands, 45
attached to promises, 89
common grace, 114n3
complexities, of change, 61–62
cross
as foundational, 48–49
multiple implications of, 35–39

depression, 57
"don't be afraid" (command), 83
Dostoevsky, F., 73

Eliot, T. S., 73
ethical discourse, and personal struggle, 92
experience, unpredictability of, 68

faith, 106–8
faith and works, 28
false teachers, 41
fear of man, 99, 101
firsthand experience, 20
forgiveness, 90–91
fruit of the Spirit, 101
future grace, 25, 30

SCRIPTURE INDEX

Scripture Index